LESSONS ON BUSINESS AND PERSONAL LEADERSHIP

FOUNDING LEADERSHIP

FROM THE MEN WHO BROUGHT YOU THE AMERICAN REVOLUTION

DR. BRENT TAYLOR

elevate

This book is lovingly dedicated to my "Founding Father," Bill Taylor. All my life you demonstrated true leadership and taught me the lifelong vision principle, "If you don't see it before you see it, you'll never see it."

CONTENTS

INTRODUCTION

"Remember that it is the actions, and not the commission, that make the Officer—and that there is more expected from him than the Title."

—George Washington addressing his officers on 8 January 1756

L EADING BY EXAMPLE is intimately linked with great leadership. So are traits and skills such as self-awareness, perseverance, clear and persuasive communication, vision-casting, and the ability to implement a vision. *Founding Leadership* profiles nine of America's "Founding Fathers," as well as Meriwether Lewis and William Clark, focusing on how each man used one key leadership tool to advance the dream of an independent and prosperous America...or, in the case of Benedict Arnold, how he squandered these talents in the service of his own ego.

This literary construct will help us better understand the importance of specific traits, and how they combine to produce effective leadership, but it's important to remember that each of the Founding Fathers was more than "just" a visionary, a vision-caster, or an influencer. None of these men were "one-trick ponies." Each combined multiple leadership qualities and abilities in a complex matrix that made him a leader in his own right.

It's not as if Benjamin Franklin was the only man capable of self-awareness at the Continental Congress; the insights he communicated to Jefferson prompted a vision to be crafted, and Jefferson planted that vision in Washington's mind so he could persuade his soldiers to attack the British lines. While compartmentalization can be a helpful tool for social scientists and historians, it's not a prescription for real-world leadership. An effective leader doesn't develop some traits and ignore others. A leader doesn't say, "Well, here's the vision. My job is done. Let someone else figure out how to make it a reality."

If the Founding Fathers had nothing but vision and no follow-through, if George Washington couldn't execute a vision, the Revolution would never have succeeded. Most of the Founders possessed all of the skills and traits discussed in this book. Washington knew how to execute a vision, as well as cast one. In addition, he displayed tremendous self-awareness, tenacity, and the ability to clearly articulate his messages.

Unfortunately, some of today's leaders seem to believe that "team effort" means they can (or should) relinquish their responsibilities to subordinates. Others try to maintain a veil of separation between their leadership roles in the business world and their off-duty lives—as if leadership were a nine-to-five undertaking with no relevance to one's personal life. "Now that I'm at home, I'll flip off my 'leadership switch' and zone out on the sofa while the kids run amok, the family dog eats the neighbor's cat, and my wife has a breakdown from trying to manage the household by herself."

In my church, I teach a class for new members about our philosophy, which illustrates the point above very nicely. In my view, the fundamental problem with Christianity in America (and this can apply to members of any faith) is the difference between a waffle and coffee.

My kids occasionally eat frozen waffles for breakfast. While they don't drown them in syrup, they are careful to fill every square. What some Christians (and some leaders) do is fill certain squares of their lives and say, "I'm going to be a Christian on Sunday and at Bible study. And I may be a Christian at my kid's football game on Saturday night, as long as the ref makes good calls. But every other day of the week is my time." Because these people often don't behave like good Christians, many non-Christians think, "What a bunch of phonies!"

What I teach is that Christians are not supposed to be like waffles, but like coffee.

When you drink coffee you don't chew the beans and then drink the hot water and then pour Sweet'N Low down your throat. You mix it all together into a perfect blend. That's what Biblical Christianity is supposed to look like. That's what effective leadership—in business and in our personal lives—is supposed to look like.

When we study men like Washington, we see that they didn't compartmentalize their lives. Their principles, their dreams, and their leadership qualities were part of who they were at the existential level. If Washington believed he wasn't living up to his leadership ideals—at home or on the battlefield—he did his best to correct the problem.

Therefore, *Founding Leadership* isn't just for office use. Nor is it only for business leaders. It was written for everyone, because at one time or another, everyone is called upon to lead. Whether we choose to accept the job is another matter, but at some point in our lives, the invitation will be extended.

Most of us will accept at least one invitation, and when we do, we will naturally look to the examples set by other leaders for inspiration and guidance, whether those examples were set by mentors or by our personal heroes from the worlds of sports, science, or history.

In my view, you can find no better role models than America's Founding Fathers. The fact that these men were flawed and fallible—that they made plenty of mistakes and endured plenty of failures—makes their accomplishments even more remarkable and their lives even more worthy of emulation.

The longer you study the words and deeds of America's Founders, the more you will see yourself in them. As remote as their lives and times may seem, the qualities that made them great live within all of us. We can awaken these qualities if we make a conscious effort to serve not just ourselves, but our families, our communities, and the world.

If great leaders are made and not born, then the next Washington, Jefferson, or Hamilton is already living among us. That person may be you.

CHAPTER ONE

BENJAMIN FRANKLIN: FIRST, KNOW THYSELF

O F ALL THE GIANTS IN THE PANTHEON of Founding Fathers, few continue to affect our lives as much as Benjamin Franklin. Many of his inventions are still in use, as are the famous sayings published in *Poor Richard's Almanac*. What's more, Franklin's presence at key moments during the Revolution helped shape the institutions that govern our lives today. The man who snatched lightning from the sky with a key and a kite was a genuine renaissance man.

Born in Boston on January 17, 1706, Benjamin Franklin was the 10th of 17 children born to Josiah and Abiah Franklin. His father, a soap and candle maker, taught him the value of industry and hard work, but dipping candles didn't interest young Benjamin. His dreams were made of grander stuff.

At 12, Franklin was apprenticed to his brother's print shop, where he learned the ways of publishing. Because his brother refused to publish Franklin's writing, Franklin adopted the pseudonym "Mrs. Silence Dogood," writing witty letters for the newspapers about the issues and people of the day. As he grew older, Franklin became ever more astute in his observations of how people behaved, thought, and lived.

After moving to Philadelphia, Franklin became a prominent citizen, publishing his own newspaper, *The Pennsylvania Gazette*. His most famous publication, however, was *Poor Richard's Almanac*, which featured colorful sayings still quoted in contemporary conversations:

- Little strokes fell great oaks. (1751)

- After crosses and losses, men grow humbler and wiser. (1737)

- Hunger never saw bad bread. (1733)

- Three may keep a secret if two of them are dead. (1735)

- Fish and visitors smell in three days. (1736)

- God helps those who help themselves. (1736)

- A good example is the best sermon. (1742)

Franklin's achievements—from lightning rods to swim flippers to bifocals—astonished the 18th-century world. To say that he was creative and innovative is an understatement. In addition to his accomplishments as an inventor, Franklin served as a printer and publisher, authoring many public letters that fueled the Revolutionary flame. He was a member of the Continental Congress, elected to the Committee of Five to draft the Declaration of Independence. He served as minister to France, Britain, and Sweden; as Postmaster General; as President of Pennsylvania (analogous to the modern position of Governor), and he negotiated the Treaty of Paris in 1783, ending the American Revolution. Franklin also organized the first volunteer fire department, charted and named the Atlantic Gulf Stream, founded the American Philosophical Society, obtained a charter for the first hospital in the United States, formed the first public lending library, and founded what is now the University of Pennsylvania.

Franklin accomplished more in one lifetime than most people can conceive of accomplishing in 10. Walter Isaacson called him "the most accomplished American of his age and the most influential in inventing the type of society America would become." There's no question that Franklin's brilliance, determination, and perseverance enabled him to accomplish much in his 84 years. However, great accomplishments are typically not attained in a vacuum. It was his understanding of people, and his lifetime of relationship building, that allowed Franklin to achieve everything he did for the American people.

Historians often wonder how great historical figures would fare today. Few doubt that Franklin would be a renowned innovator and "thought leader," no matter when he lived.

WHAT PERSONAL IDENTITY MEANS
FOR LEADERSHIP

Given all of the above, Franklin hardly seems the sort of man to experience an identity crisis. But that's precisely what Franklin endured at a pivotal moment in his life and the life of the new nation. In fact, had it not been for this "dark night of the soul," Franklin might not have cast his lot with the band of rebellious malcontents we now call the Founding Fathers.

Before we address Franklin's defining moment—an event that compelled the celebrity inventor, newspaper mogul, and statesmen to risk his reputation, his fortune, and his life on a seemingly hopeless rebellion against the world's greatest superpower, let's examine the nature of personal identity and what it means for leadership.

WHAT IS PERSONAL IDENTITY?

The basic answer to that question is that personal identity is the tales we tell ourselves to define (1) who we are and (2) our role in the world. We create identity by organizing our experiences (actually, the memories of our experiences) into one or more narratives. In turn, these narratives are condensed into role titles and/or role descriptions such as father and husband, president and CEO, team player, morally upright person, stamp collector, or fantasy-football enthusiast. These labels are the quick self-definitions we use to distinguish ourselves from others. They help us make sense of who we are and where we belong. They can also provide a sense of self-worth, mission, and purpose.

Obviously, leaders must know who they are to understand where they're going, but the issue goes deeper than that. There are two types of identity that we all deal with: positional identity and personal identity.

"I'm the governor. I'm the mayor. I'm the boss. I'm the dad."

Positional identity addresses activities and roles. It describes your position relative to others by pinpointing your roles, functions, and activities, as well as the organizations to which you belong and the causes you champion. "I'm a Baptist. I'm a weekend fisherman. I'm a community volunteer." Positional identity describes what you do, not who you really are.

Personal identity is about deeper self-knowledge. It describes who you are vis-à-vis abstract ideas that include values, purposes, and missions. It's often difficult to communicate your personal identity in a single word or pithy phrase.

Many people confuse positional and personal identity because they don't have a firm grasp on who they are at the deepest levels. For this reason, most of us think in terms of positional identity if we think about the issue at all. "I'm an administrative assistant. I'm a golf caddy. I'm an animal rights advocate. That's who I am." Again, positional identity describes what you do, not who you really are. Many organizations confuse positional identity and personal identity, if they even bother to address this issue (and many don't). They think in terms of what they produce, not why they produce it. "We make milk products. We make computers. We disseminate our clients' messages through public relations strategies and tactics." These positional identities don't define what the organizations really are and why they produce these particular products or services.

Not long ago, I watched a TED Talk featuring Simon Sinek, who spoke about the "Golden Circles." At the center of three concentric circles he drew was the word "why." Outside this inner circle was anoth-

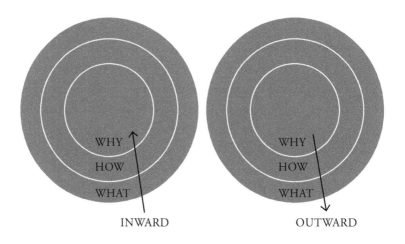

INWARD   OUTWARD

er circle featuring the word "how," and the outermost circle was labeled "what."

According to Sinek, most companies tackle the issue of identity from the outside inward.

They ask:

1. What are we going to do? (We'll make computers.)

2. How are we going to make them? (We'll make them this way.)

3. Why are we going to do this? (This question is rarely answered.)

What separates companies such as Apple (which recently surpassed Coke as the No. 1 brand worldwide) from businesses and organizations that work the "inward" process on the concentric circles is that Steve Jobs began his quest for organizational identity with the inner ring of the circles.

The first question Jobs sought to answer was the most important anyone can ask: *why.*

1. Why are we doing this? (We want to make life better for people.)

2. How are we going to do it? (We'll make well-designed, easy-to-use computers.)

3. What are we making? (Mac, iPad, iPhone, etc.)

Too many leaders define their lives and purposes in the same way as the first organization: "This is what I do, and this is how I do it." *Why* never enters the picture.

Creating a personal identity must begin with ***why***. It must begin with understanding *why you exist* before moving to what to do next and how.

Leading others requires that you first understand yourself—that you first develop a baseline self-awareness. Self-awareness allows you to honestly assess your strengths and weaknesses, and honestly assess those of the people and organizations you work with. There's no such thing as effective leadership without people skills, and mastering people skills begins with self-awareness—understanding the identity of the person that is *you*.

Although Ben Franklin had a gift for self-awareness, he didn't settle on a strong, fixed identity until surprisingly late in his life. Once he made that choice, however, he became—almost overnight—one of the most radical and influential champions of the American independence movement.

FRANKLIN'S "DARK NIGHT OF THE SOUL"

By the time of the Boston Tea Party in December 1774, Franklin had acquired a positional identity that would be the envy of every wannabe celebrity on *American Idol*, *X Factor*, or *Keeping up With the Kardashians*. By today's standards, Ben Franklin was bigger than the Beatles. As fate would have it, though, his personal identity was resting on quicksand.

It's important to note that, hitherto, Franklin was thoroughly invested in the success of the British Empire. He identified as a British citizen first and an American second.

With the exception of George III, Franklin was the most famous man in the Empire—a household name across the Western Hemisphere. He was also a British official (though not formally). For almost 18 years, he'd represented America's interests to the British government as the London agent of Pennsylvania and Massachusetts—i.e., he was a lobbyist. Moreover, Franklin's son William was then the Royal Governor of New Jersey.

Two decades earlier, Franklin had proposed the "Albany Plan," which envisioned a central government for the 13 colonies, headed by a crown-appointed president. As late as 1774, he sought to make America an equal political partner of Great Britain. If he had seen his dearest wish realized, a new symbol would have graced the Union Jack—one representing the 13 *united* American colonies. His dream was a United Kingdom composed of England, Scotland, Ireland, *and* the American colonies. He didn't envision or *want* a politically independent America. His hope was that America would grow, expand, and evolve within the British Empire.

As the agent for Massachusetts and Pennsylvania, and because of his fame and renowned intellect, Franklin's advice on all things American was frequently sought in London's highest circles. So when riots and boycotts broke out across the colonies in response to the Stamp Act (1765), it was to Franklin that London's power elite turned for explanations and solutions. As crisis followed crisis from 1765 to 1775, the best and brightest in British government repeatedly turned to Franklin for advice and counsel. During these years, however, Franklin gradually lost touch with the worldviews and wishes of his New World brethren—a trend that eventually proved disastrous to his career in British politics. With his fingers off the pulse of colonial opinion, Franklin's pronouncements proved wrong more often than right.

Matters finally came to a head after the Boston Tea Party in December 1773.

When this news arrived in London in January 1774, Franklin confronted the biggest crisis of his career. Having been called upon again and again to explain the actions of the colonists, as tensions and violence escalated, Franklin was running out of rational explanations for why Americans thought and behaved as they did. He was also running out of ways to explain the actions of the British government to his constituents back home. In short, Franklin found himself between a rock and a hard place.

His solution to this predicament was a clever one—far too clever for his own good.

He decided to leak a number of letters that had been passed to him by a third party whose identity remains unknown to this day. The letters, written by Governor Thomas Hutchinson of Massachusetts and Peter Oliver, Hutchinson's lieutenant governor, essentially said that, because of the increasing violence in America, the liberties of the American people should be suppressed—at least temporarily. Franklin believed that if these letters were made public, Americans and the British government would blame the rising discontent on misguided officials such as Hutchinson, who were conspiring to deprive Americans of their rights as Englishmen.

Franklin guessed correctly that if the letters went public, there would be rioting in the colonies. What he failed to anticipate, though, is the uproar that also occurred in London—one that crippled his reputation and status. In an age when honor was everything, London's elite castigated Franklin for violating the obligations and responsibilities of a gentleman. Gentlemen did not steal and publicize other people's mail. (Note: to suggest someone was *not* a gentleman in the 18th century was the equivalent of calling someone a slack-jawed, ignorant barbarian.)

In London, the terms of the debate shifted. Instead of arguing the merits (or lack thereof) of the Patriots' demands, British officials vented their fury on Franklin as the most visible and influential representative of America. In short order, Franklin was hauled before the British Privy Council, the group that legislated for the colonies, where Franklin was required to stand in the dock as the Solicitor General Alexander Wedderburn, chief prosecutor of King George, vilified him in the most vitriolic terms, claiming that he was a traitor and an ingrate, he was not a gentleman, he did not have the British Empire's interest in mind and not even the interest of the Americans in mind, but was thinking only of his own personal advancement.

People who were present at this session of Wedderburn's attack, which was so slanderous that no newspaper in London would print an account of it, assumed that Franklin was humiliated. Most of them figured that if they were in that situation they, too, would be humiliated.

I don't think so. My interpretation is that Franklin wasn't humiliated, he was outraged. He believed that the King's solicitor, this hired-gun lawyer, had no right to treat him the way he was treating him. Furthermore, he was being criticized for being what—for being an American?

It's a bit of an exaggeration, I think, but maybe not too much, to say that this was the moment of decision for Franklin. When he realized that all these years he'd been thinking of himself as an Englishman, as a Briton, he wasn't being allowed to be a first-class Briton. So therefore, he would have to be an American. *Franklin walked into that session on the morning of January 29, 1774, as an Englishman—and walked out an American.*

If one of the principal chores of Franklin's life was to determine his identity—was he a Bostonian? Was he a Philadelphian? Was he a Briton? Was he an American?—on this morning in 1774, Franklin realized what the answer was. *First and foremost, he was an American.*[1]

Months later, after a subsequent attempt to argue the American cause before Parliament (in partnership with Lord Howe, who later became the commander-in-chief of British forces in America) ended in yet another humiliation, Franklin noted:

> *I was much disgusted from the ministerial side by many base reflections on American courage, religion, understanding, etc., in which we were treated with the utmost contempt, as the lowest of mankind, almost of a different species from the English of Britain. But particularly American honesty was abused by some of the lords, who asserted that we were all knaves and wanted only by this dispute to avoid paying our debts—that if we had any sense of equity or justice we should offer payment of the tea [referring to the tea of the Boston Tea Party].*[2]

When Franklin finally returned to the colonies in 1775, he was out of touch with what was happening. By the time he took his seat at the Continental Congress in Philadelphia, therefore, some of his colleagues privately questioned his dedication to the cause. Had he not spent the previous 18 years living in England, trying to negotiate compromises between the increasingly divergent interests and desires of two peoples? Could he really be trusted? Wasn't Franklin at best a lukewarm revolutionary?

To the surprise of many in Congress, Franklin's insider knowledge of what had been happening in England over the past two decades transformed him into one of *the most zealous and radical* of the rebels. He had seen the extent to which British politics (in his view) had been corrupted. Between this and his raking over the coals by Wedderburn, Franklin now believed the American colonies must separate from Britain. He advocated independence at a time when most members of Congress (other than John Adams) dared not even contemplate the idea of independence.

STRONG IDENTITY = CLEARER VISION

The moment Franklin ceased to walk that tightrope between his dueling personal identities—British citizen and American patriot—his vision cleared almost instantly, and he became one of the most zealous of the Founders. Without the rose-colored glasses he'd worn for so long, he immediately understood the path he should follow. In short, by answering the question, "Who am I and *why?*" he cleared the clutter from his vision and swept every mental obstacle from his path of action.

Like Franklin before age 68, many leaders and organizations today understand *what they do*, but not *who* they are and *why* they are pursuing the current course. "Who and why" are questions as fundamental to effective leadership as "to be or not to be."

Personal identity fosters self-awareness—the ability to recognize your strengths and weaknesses and the benefits you can offer to the community. Recognizing your own strengths and weaknesses makes it possible to identify with, and team with, like-minded people who have complementary talents and skills. Recognizing the benefits you can offer to the community makes it possible to devote yourself and your organization to a cause that is larger and more inspirational than your narrow self-interests. Only by satisfactorily answering the *why* question can you communicate a vision that will transcend the mundane and the "me too"—the bland, forgettable, wall-plaque "mission statements" decorating the lobbies and websites of every Brand X company across the globe.

The leader without a strong personal identity is like a ship without a rudder: You will wind up sailing all over the map, depending on which way the wind is blowing.

Recently, a friend spoke at a conference at which the topic of identity was discussed. During the Q&A session, an audience member raised her hand and asked, "Has anybody ever been to Caracas?" Several people raised their hands. She went on to explain that Caracas has express buses *galore*. These buses don't travel for a half-mile before the first stop, but drive hours and hours before the first stop. It would be unwise, therefore, for an uninformed traveler to hop on a particular bus, thinking, "I'll get off in a few minutes if I find that I chose the wrong bus." The buses venture to every part of the country, so you have to be sure of your destination before stepping aboard. If you don't know where you're going in Caracas, any old bus will do.

This same logic applies to leadership—to the leader's need to discover and fulfill a larger purpose and mission for himself and the organization by tapping into a deeper personal identity.

If you don't know who you are, you can't know where you're going. Any old bus will do. It really doesn't matter which one you take because you're not going anywhere in particular. Okay, you're going somewhere in particular, but you're not in control of the final destination.

If you are a real student of leadership (and life) you will, according to the ancient inscription on the Temple of Apollo at Delphi, *know thyself*. An understanding of self is the real gateway to understanding others. For Franklin, knowing himself and mastering the desired qualities of life was a lifelong quest. From his earliest days until his final breath, he sought to defeat vices that would hinder his abilities, and enhance virtues that would advance his achievements. As a student of life, Franklin was first and foremost a student of *himself*.

There is no clearer example of Franklin's study of his own life than his autobiography. Written over the course of several years, it contains both the facts of his life and an imagined "self"—a self largely based on desires but not realities.

In the autobiography, Franklin tells the history of his life mixed with the reputation he wants to have. The work was supposed to be a personal story for his family, but Franklin was savvy enough to know he was writing for a much larger audience. Filled with fact and fiction,

The Autobiography of Benjamin Franklin is a revealing chronicle of comments and observations about Franklin's life and his views on that life.

Outlined in the autobiography is a collection of 13 life virtues. Franklin stressed self-mastery in all things, and these moral virtues spelled out what he determined to hold dear. He believed that these virtues would foster "moral perfection." Included in the collection are:

- Temperance: Eat not to dullness, drink not to elevation.

- Silence: Speak not but what may benefit others or yourself. Avoid trifling conversation.

- Order: Let all your things have their places. Let each part of your business have its time.

- Frugality: Make no expense but to do good to others or yourself (a veiled reference to Romans 13:8).

- Industry: Lose no time. Be always employed in something useful. Cut off all unnecessary actions.

By practicing these virtues, Franklin believed he could master himself and the passions that raged within. He valued the fact that he could command himself to accomplish what he deemed "moral perfection," though he didn't seem to value moral perfection for its own sake. In fact, he would rarely forgo something that might lead to personal pleasure. However, he frequently commented on this and the other weaknesses that so easily entangled him. In fact, some of Franklin's best advice sprang from his own unfulfilled desire to achieve self-mastery.

"What you seem to be, be really."

"If passion drives you, let reason hold the reins."

THE KISS OF DEATH

Former Chrysler Chairman Lee Iacocca once said, "Anyone who doesn't get along with people has earned the kiss of death...because all we have around here are people."

Understanding people is more than just a helpful soft skill; it is vital to effective relationship-building in both your professional and personal life. A skilled leader understands that, while an organization may produce and sell widgets, its most important resource is people. The leader with strong abilities to relate to individuals, a clear understanding of what motivates people, and the aptitudes necessary to encourage, inspire, and lead them will be effective in every endeavor.

Consider these two statistics:

- According to the Carnegie Foundation, about 15 percent of one's success is due to technical knowledge, while 85 percent is due to one's skill in human engineering—i.e., the ability to get along with and lead people.[3]

- About 80 percent of the people who fail at work do so for one reason: They do not relate well to other people.[4]

It's easy to see the value of applying emotional intelligence to better understand people, as well as mastering people skills. Whether it's in your personal relationships with family and friends or in multi-million-dollar business deals, life is inescapably human. Great leaders understand this and seek to develop relationships that are both intimate and lasting.

Margaret Wheatley once said, "Relationships are all there is. Everything in the universe only exists because it is in relationship to everything else. Nothing exists in isolation. We have to stop pretending we are individuals that can go it alone."[5] Or, as John Donne famously said, "No man is an island, entire of itself..."

Franklin not only knew this, he believed it to his core, living his life in a way that maximized his understanding of people. It was this understanding that, more than anything else, helped him to seal an alliance with the French in 1778—a partnership that tilted the odds of victory decidedly in the Patriots' favor.

From the moment he stepped onto French soil, Franklin sought to nurture long-term relationships with the King and the influential courtiers of Versailles. He began by cultivating an image that was calculated to surprise and delight the "movers and shakers" of the aristocracy. He sought to meet (and, whenever possible, exceed) their expectations of what an American "backwoods" philosopher should be. And in almost every respect, Franklin delivered what the French wanted: he donned rustic clothes topped with a coonskin cap, he issued words of wit and wisdom on the rare occasions when he spoke (in barely intelligible) French, he remained agreeable and affable at all times, and (most importantly) he knew exactly when to lobby hard for the American agenda and when to bide his time.

Even the irascible John Adams—perhaps *the least people-oriented* diplomat America ever sent abroad—was forced to admit that Franklin's "shtick" was instrumental in furthering the American cause at Versailles.

Whatever Franklin's failings and flaws, Adams never discounted the value of his popularity and prestige. French esteem for the "good doctor" remained of immense importance to the American cause, as Adams knew.

What most distressed Adams about Franklin was his approach with French foreign minister Charles Gravier, comte de Vergennes. He "hates to offend and seldom gives any opinion till obliged," Adams noted. "Although he has as determined a soul as any man, yet it is his constant policy never to say yes or no decidedly but when he cannot avoid it." Franklin's concept of diplomacy was to ask for nothing that Vergennes would not give, be grateful for whatever help the French provided, and remain ever accommodating and patient. As Franklin's friend Condorcet remarked approvingly, Franklin as a diplomat "observed much and acted little."[6]

FORGE EMOTIONAL CONNECTIONS

In short, what Adams considered flaws, his French counterparts considered strengths.

Had Adams been chief envoy to France, it's entirely possible that we Americans would speak with British accents today. While the always-social Franklin ingratiated himself with his hosts by immersing himself in their "decadent" lifestyles, the impatient, all-business-all-the-time Adams stuck out like a puritanical thumb, as likely to insult his French counterparts as flatter them. While Adams relied heavily on abstract reason and logical argument to persuade people to his points of view, Franklin built lasting relationships by forging *emotional connections*—a powerful tool in any era, and one that often spells the difference between success and failure.

Consider this tale of two wars: World War II and Vietnam. Why did one enjoy overwhelming public support while the other divided popular opinion? One could list a thousand reasons, but one difference is obvious. During the Second World War, Franklin Roosevelt made sure every American understood the stakes involved in the conflict—that everyone knew this was a life-and-death struggle. Moreover, he took steps to ensure that every citizen was emotionally connected and invested in a successful outcome. More importantly, he made sure that every American *believed* he could make a positive difference. There were scrap metal drives and paper drives; people were organized into civil defense forces; food and fuel were rationed. Those who couldn't serve in the armed forces felt they could contribute to victory on the home front. Everyone was told—and *shown*—that their contributions mattered. The nation's emotional focus was directed toward "V for Victory" and Rosie the Riveter.

By contrast, Lyndon Johnson didn't come close to securing a positive emotional connection for the Vietnam War. Quite the opposite: He succeeded in generating widespread negative emotions about the war—likely because he didn't clearly spell out America's war aims. Few people had any idea what victory would look like, how it would benefit them, and why they should care (unless they were likely to be drafted). This era also marked a notable shift in how the media viewed the presidency and administration officials—reporters were deceived and bought into it, and when the facts came to light, reporters and editors lost much of their previous respect for officials.

Without clarity and compelling emotional reasons to fight in Vietnam, there was a lack of team spirit on the home front—to put it mildly.

Conversely, the efforts FDR spearheaded on the home front encouraged people to participate in the war effort, regardless of how significant each person's contribution really was. People really felt as though they were making a difference. They had a stake in the outcome of the conflict, whereas during Vietnam civilians were told to go about their business as if nothing was happening and let the professionals worry about the sacrificing and dying. Civilians, therefore, did not have to "buy in" to whether the war was just or righteous—or even a good idea—because most weren't called upon to make any contributions or decisions. Emotional connections were not forged; therefore, people did not care about their level (or lack) of involvement.

SEARCH OTHERS FOR VIRTUES; SEARCH YOURSELF FOR VICES

When I visit with people about getting married, I talk about everyone's search for Mr. or Ms. Right. I tell couples that marriage is not about finding the right person, but about *being* the right person. You can choose to be Mr. Right or Ms. Right.

In choosing an identity, you can choose to say, "I'm going to be driven. I'm going to be focused. I'm going to accomplish my goals, but I'm not going to harm people in the process. Instead, I'm going to lead people."

Without knowing who you are, it's easy to fall over the fine line that separates passion for a cause from obsession with a cause. It's all too easy to morph from Anakin Skywalker to Darth Vader or, in real life, from Maximilian Robespierre the reformer and idealistic revolutionary to Robespierre of *The Terror*—someone who's come to think of himself as a god—someone who believes, *I am the revolution. Anyone who dares oppose my will must be crushed as an enemy of my vision.*

One of Franklin's virtues was his recognition that he fully recognized his weaknesses. Although he sometimes embraced the weaknesses more than he embraced the virtues, he knew *who* he was, what he believed, and where he was failing. This understanding required a degree of introspection and honest evaluation that most people don't pursue—much less achieve. The reason most people fail to truly know themselves is that their focus is on finding fault in others. Again, we would be wise to heed Franklin's advice: "Search others for their virtues, thyself for thy vices." (*Poor Richards Almanac*, 1738).

Self-awareness increases your understanding of relationships, which in turn helps you develop stronger interpersonal skills. Good leadership requires a thorough understanding of people, their personality types, and their motivations. This isn't theory. It's fact. You cannot inspire people with a vision—no matter how clear, carefully crafted, and compelling it may seem in your own mind—if you don't understand the people you hope to persuade and motivate.

CHAPTER TWO
THOMAS JEFFERSON: A MAN OF VISION

IN 1962, OVER A WHITE HOUSE DINNER with living Nobel recipients, President John F. Kennedy famously quipped, "I think this is the most extraordinary collection of talent, of human knowledge, that has ever been gathered together at the White House, with the possible exception of when Thomas Jefferson dined alone." Few men have possessed the raw intellect, talent, and vision of our nation's third president, Thomas Jefferson.

Jefferson was born April 13, 1743, outside of Charlottesville, Virginia. His family was wealthy and well-known, and his parents displayed extraordinary talents, which they bequeathed to the young Jefferson. His formal education included Latin, Greek, and the violin (a lifelong love), while his informal education included farming, surveying, and cartography.

After attending the College of William and Mary in Williamsburg, Jefferson became an accomplished attorney at law, winning most of his cases and earning a reputation as wise beyond his years. During this time, he married the love of his life, Martha Wayles Skelton, who would bear him six children—though only two would survive to adulthood.

Amidst the tumultuous events leading to the American Revolution, Jefferson rose in political power, elected by Virginia to attend the Second Continental Congress. There he was elected to the Committee of Five charged with drafting a Declaration of Independence. Clearly a talented writer, Jefferson was given the charge of writing the now-sacred document while the rest of the committee would make edits before presenting the document to the Congress.

Later, Jefferson served as Governor of Virginia and Secretary of State in the George Washington administration. Following a vicious and ugly election against his former friend (and second President) John Adams, he became the new nation's third commander-in-chief.

As president, Jefferson oversaw many changes, including the milestone transfer of power from one party (the Federalists of Washington, Hamilton, and Adams) to another (Jefferson's Democratic-Republican party). He also had the great foresight and fortune to acquire the land we call the Louisiana Purchase. Jefferson's years in the presidency helped seal the new nation's hold—and more than doubled its land size.

As the founder of the University of Virginia, governor of his home state, writer of the Declaration of Independence and the Virginia Statute for Religious Freedom, the "sage of Monticello" will be forever revered as a man of great courage and inspiring vision.

AN OVERUSED BUZZWORD

Throughout American culture, and the business world in particular, no single word is abused as often as *vision*. The term has become a key ingredient in every buzzword salad tossed by corporate management gurus, consultants, and motivational speakers, robbing it of meaning and vitality. So bad have things become that *Forbes* recently translated "*I'm a bit of a visionary*" as "I'm a bit of an egomaniac and narcissist."

(Companion clichés on the *Forbes* list include "*It's a paradigm shift*" = "I don't know what's going on in our business, but we're not making as much money as we used to," and "*Let's ballpark this*" = "Let's shoot around a bunch of ideas since we have no clue what to do.")[7]

Given the tawdry state of affairs, I doubt this single chapter will restore *vision* to its once-exalted status. But since we have nothing to lose, let's start by debunking some common myths about vision.

Myth No. 1: Everybody sees what you see. If you ask the CEO of a typical company, "What is your vision for the company?" he'll explain it. If you ask, "How many people in your organization can communicate the vision?" he will probably say, "Everybody." In my experience, very few employees can articulate the leader's vision. If you ask 50 employees "What is the company's vision?" you'll receive 50 different responses—or blank stares.

Myth No. 2: I have clearly communicated the vision. Goals, objectives, and tasks do not a vision make. "A vision without a task is but a dream, a task without a vision is drudgery, a vision *with* a task is the hope of the world."[8] Many leaders set short-term goals—e.g., increasing fourth-quarter profits. Some leaders set long-term goals—e.g., capturing enough market share to dominate Industry X. However, it is relatively rare for a boss to communicate a clear and compelling vision that strikes an emotional chord with internal and external stakeholders: "We will improve the health and nutrition of every American by making the highest-quality, best-tasting packaged foods."

Goals and objectives are not vision; they are tasks: the means to achieving a vision. Assuming the leader has defined the vision—and many don't—it's up to that leader to broadcast it to anyone who will listen. Employees, vendors, shareholders, customers, prospective customers: they must all understand the vision. And they can't do that unless they hear it...over and over and over.

One thing I've learned as a leader: By the time people start "getting it," you will be nearly nauseated from having to reiterate the vision so many times. The message will start sinking in only when you, as the leader, are sick of talking about it.

Myth No. 3: Everyone is a visionary. Wrong. For one thing, vision is something that distinguishes leaders from followers. For another, I've met *plenty* of people without vision—boatloads of them. "I just want to be left alone to have fun on the weekends" is a common refrain among employees. In fact, surprisingly few people ever develop a vision—one that serves a larger cause, whether that cause is mentoring children, feeding the homeless, digging wells in Africa, designing an app to help people lose weight, or reorganizing companies to unleash the creative potential of workers. Most people drift through their professional and personal lives. They just float. Not only are they not visionaries, they're not seeking a vision, and they aren't interested in finding one. For leaders, this is deadly. As Proverbs 29:18 (KJV) says, "Where there is no vision, the people perish."

COMMUNICATING VISION

Clearly communicating your vision is an art form. It is the art of painting an emotionally compelling picture of the way things *could* be. As an example, consider the following passage from Jefferson's 1801 inaugural address, delivered in the wake of perhaps the most vicious presidential campaign ever fought. (Compared with the no-holds-barred brawl between Jefferson and John Adams, the 2016 campaign between Barack Obama and Mitt Romney was a tepid affair. In the minds of Federalists and Democratic-Republicans, nothing less than the survival of the American republic was at stake.)

> *...every difference of opinion is not a difference of principle. We have called by different names brethren of the same principle. We are all Republicans, we are all Federalists. If there be any among us who would wish to dissolve this Union or to change its republican form, let them stand undisturbed as monuments of the safety with which error of opinion may be tolerated where reason is left free to combat it. I know, indeed, that some honest men fear that a republican government can not be strong, that this Government is not strong enough; but would the honest patriot, in the full tide of successful experiment, abandon a government which has so far kept us free and firm on the theoretic and visionary fear that this Government, the world's best hope, may by possibility want energy to preserve itself? I trust not. I believe this, on the contrary, is the strongest Government on earth. I believe it is the only one where every man, at the call of the law, would fly to the standard of the law, and would meet invasions of the public order as his own personal concern. Sometimes it is said that man can not be trusted with the government of himself. Can he, then, be trusted with the government of others? Or have we found angels in the forms of kings to govern him? Let history answer this question.*[9]

Jefferson communicated his powerful vision by establishing an emotional connection with people, something that requires keen awareness, as well as empathy. Most importantly, he communicated stakes that *truly mattered* to his audience. This is vital to inspiring an audience. You must spread the vision in ways that motivate audiences to throw off their jackets, roll up their sleeves, jump on the bandwagon, and stay on that wagon until the dream is realized.

The most compelling vision is not tied to promises of rewards or punishments. Grand visions are linked with a higher purpose. They represent meaningful dreams beyond the mundane; something more noble than self-interested pursuits. Provided you communicate it clearly and make an emotional connection, a worthwhile vision will stir within your followers a powerful desire to accomplish that really big thing.

Talk of profits, share prices, and quarterly growth is unlikely to inspire many people. These things are goals—not a vision. Although goals can arouse short-term motivation, they won't transform uninspired drones into true believers or tireless champions.

Uninspired leaders tend to drone on about employee "buy-in," "teamwork," and "growth" without answering key questions such as "Why should anyone care about working on this particular team?" (beyond the paycheck) and "What does 'growth' mean to everyone?" Uninspired leaders are also in love with mission statements—statements so vague and syrupy that they read like the parody Miss America speech from Woody Allen's *Sleeper:* "I would use my title to bring peace to all nations of the world, be it black, be they white, be it whatever."

From employees' point of view, all this talk about buy-in, teamwork, and growth does nothing to spark deep passion. It certainly doesn't appeal to the "better angels of our nature." Why is buy-in important? What role does it play in the larger vision? What does growth mean to people who aren't paid six figures, and may not care about climbing the ladder—data entry clerks, administrative assistants, and receptionists? Why should they care about teamwork and growth? What value will the vision add to the lives of employees, customers, and members of the community?

Most Americans don't own stock, and aren't interested in climbing very far up the corporate ladder. If the boss communicates his vision to only a handful of elite stakeholders, ignoring everyone in the trenches, he's not selling a vision—he's selling patronage. Can you imagine what would have happened if George Washington had done nothing but talk about the money, land, and titles he would grant the officers after the war, ignoring the common soldiers? How much revolutionary zeal and fighting spirit would this have generated among the troops? "Help me whip the British, men, and you'll get a 50-dollar bonus, assuming you survive."

I was recently invited to speak to employees of WhiteWave Food Products in Boulder, Colorado. (The company produces Horizon organic milk, Silk dairy alternatives and juice blends, and Land O'Lakes butter, among other products.) Before my speech, my contact said to me, "Our CEO wants you to help our employees. He doesn't care if it contributes a penny to the bottom line. He wants us to help our employees."

The more I learned about the company—about their core values, guiding principles, and goals—the more convinced I became of the absolute necessity of sharing vision: from the farmers to the C-Suite, everyone must share the same vision and desires. "People here are more passionate about organic food than they are about their next paycheck," said my contact. *This* is the vision that WhiteWave employees have bought into. *This* is what inspires people to persevere.

I had the privilege of sharing with the employees of this great company how they can not only manage stressful situations, but also thrive under pressure. Like in all companies, the employees of WhiteWave are searching for tools to help them navigate life and, I hope, the goal of the CEO to improve the lives of the employees was met that day.

JEFFERSON DECLARES HIS MOST COMPELLING VISION

Thinking of Thomas Jefferson and the Declaration of Independence, many of us regard it as "one of those few quasi-religious episodes in American history, that moment when...a solitary Jefferson was allowed a glimpse of the eternal truths and then offered the literary inspiration to inscribe them on the American soul. From mid-May to early July 1776, Jefferson wrote the words that made him famous and that, over the course of the next two centuries, associated him with the most visionary version of the American dream."[10]

I won't deny that Jefferson's words may have been divinely inspired, but it's important to view the man and his ideas in the proper context, lest we believe he drew his inspiration from thin air. None of his thoughts were formed in isolation or in a historical vacuum, though their expression was uniquely Jefferson's.

By the time Jefferson sat down to draft the Declaration, the decision to separate from Great Britain was a foregone conclusion in the minds of many members of the Congress. Thomas Paine's *Common Sense* (published in January 1776) had electrified the colonists, for the first time sparking a widespread belief that Americans could be, and should be, an independent nation. The previously unthinkable had become not just thinkable, but inevitable. Add to this the writings of John Locke, Montesquieu, and John Adams, as well as Jefferson's previous writing (the Virginia State Constitution and *Summary View*), and we see that Jefferson had plenty of "background material" to work with.

The foundation of the republic was already being laid. What it lacked was a document that combined the emotional appeals of *Common Sense* and the philosophical framework for a national government like that outlined in *Thought on Government*. After all, even if many colonists were ready to fight and die for their independence, they wanted an idea of what independence would bring them after the revolution.

The war had been raging for more than a year, and things weren't going well for the Patriots. British fleets had been sighted off the coasts of New York and South Carolina, and an American expeditionary force to Canada had met with humiliating defeat. More than ever, the Patriots needed a vision that would inspire them to persevere in the face of what would surely be a long and costly conflict.

Inspiration is precisely what Jefferson delivered in the Declaration as a whole. But it is the 58 words below that have become the most famous, and rightly so. They are "one of the most quoted statements of human rights in recorded history, as well as the most eloquent justification of revolution on behalf of them." The words reflect Jefferson's visionary genius, demonstrating how one individual can inspire millions of people for generations afterward. The passage is one of the few that survived editing by the Continental Congress without comment and with very few changes:

> *We hold these truths to be self evident; that all men are created equal; that they are endowed by their Creator with certain [inherent and] inalienable Rights; that among these are life, liberty, and the pursuit of happiness; that to secure these rights, governments are instituted among men, deriving their just powers from the consent of the governed.*[11]

Copies of the Declaration of Independence were quickly printed and distributed across the country, where they were read and discussed by individual citizens and soldiers, or read aloud in town squares, taverns, and churches. When the Declaration arrived in George Washington's camp, he personally read the document aloud before the assembled troops, so they would understand exactly what they were now fighting for.

If Lexington and Concord was the "shot heard round the world," the Declaration of Independence contained the words heard round the world. Jefferson's vision would inspire Americans to suffer through seven more years of hardship and privation, and his messages, two decades later, would help inspire the French to overthrow their thousand-year-old monarchy.

You will probably never write words as famous as the Declaration of Independence, but it's imperative that you articulate a compelling vision for your organization or your family. What's at stake is not your country's freedom, but your organization's future. Jefferson found his voice in the Declaration of Independence. Your voice must speak to your family's or organization's future.

THE FOUR PARTS OF VISION

Vision consists of four parts: *hindsight, sight, foresight,* and *insight.* Hindsight requires that you examine the past, sight enables you to see everything around you, and foresight lets you intuit future possibilities and pathways. What connects hindsight, sight, and foresight to create a complete vision is *insight.* More than anything else, vision requires insight, allowing you to analyze past and present, predict future possibilities, and then develop strategies and tactics to execute the dream. Getting from here to there also includes these three processes:

1. *Awareness:* You must be aware of the possibilities and pathways for success. You must know where you are, where you've been, and where you're going.

2. *Attitude:* Attitude is everything, especially when it comes to vision. You must realistically evaluate the risks and possible outcomes. You must evaluate the strengths and weaknesses of possible pathways to success. You must also evaluate your willingness to see the vision through. If you aren't willing to do what it takes to realize the vision, your effort will be wasted.

3. *Action:* You must follow through on the vision, sharing the wealth as well as the risks. For me, successful action boils down to five things: execution, execution, execution, plus perseverance and courage.

Leadership requires that you understand who you are and where you are, where your organization is, where your family is, where your community is, and where the nation is. From there, you need to paint a compelling picture of what the future could (or should) look like. That's what vision-casting is. It's about painting a compelling picture.

To illustrate vision-casting in action, we need look no further than Thomas Jefferson's purchase of the Louisiana Territory in 1803.

Though he never traveled farther west than Virginia's Shenandoah Valley, Jefferson was fascinated by the American West—the lands stretching from the Ohio River Valley to the Mississippi Valley and beyond. He'd been aware of their strategic importance and potential, in terms of resources and arable land, since the 1780s when he first proposed an expedition led by George Rogers Clark, the brother of William Clark. So concerned was he about the strategic importance of the trans-Mississippi West to future American expansion that, as secretary of state under Washington, he was prepared to risk war to prevent England or France from taking control of the Louisiana Territory. (Spain was largely an "absentee landlord," whereas England or France would likely put "boots on the ground" to assert their sovereignty.)

Jefferson had a vision of a United States that extended far beyond the East Coast. He had a vision of the United States as a transcontinental empire—an "empire of liberty." He was perfectly aware of what European powers had done over the centuries to exert influence or outright ownership over swaths of North America, and he stayed current with their latest maneuvers and machinations.

He was aware of the economic and strategic possibilities the new land promised, as well as the best pathways for U.S. expansion. One of the literal pathways, he believed, would be an all-water route stretching from Washington, D.C. to the Pacific—from the Potomac to the Ohio to the Mississippi to the Missouri. (As Lewis and Clark learned the hard way, though, a navigable all-water route from Atlantic to Pacific did not exist.)

When rumors reached Jefferson in 1802 that Spain had transferred ownership of the Louisiana Territory to Napoleon and France, Jefferson instantly saw the shift in the strategic situation, recognizing the French threat to American security and expansion.

The sale of the Louisiana region to France was, he thought, a major disaster that "completely reverses all the political relations of the United States and will form a new epoch in our political course." Jefferson believed it constituted the greatest challenge to American independence and national integrity since the American Revolution. "There is on the globe one single spot, the possessor of which is our natural and habit-ual enemy," he explained to Robert R. Livingston, U.S. Ambassador to France. That epicenter of American national interest was New Orleans. Despite past friendship with France and despite his own personal affini-ty for the Franco-American alliance, the moment France occupied New Orleans the two nations must have become mortal enemies. "From that moment," he concluded ominously, "we must marry ourselves to the British fleet and nation." Given his deep and lifelong hatred of England, Jefferson was effectively describing French control of the Mississippi as the equivalent of an international earthquake that moved all the geolog-ical templates into a new pattern.[12]

Knowing that most Americans favored expansion, he took immedi-ate action, sending James Monroe (then governor of Virginia) to France as a special envoy, and authorizing him to negotiate the purchase of New Orleans and as much of the Mississippi Valley as possible.

While negotiations were under way during the winter and spring of 1803, Jefferson displayed a "get tough" attitude toward this threat to American security, reinforcing his attitude with skillfully leaked infor-mation and strategic actions. He made sure an old French friend, du Pont de Nemours, was given information about Jefferson's serious in-tent—information that could be leaked to the proper officials in France. And when Spanish officials still in charge of New Orleans abruptly closed the port to American shipping, Jefferson remained calm in the face of growing pressure to send a military expedition to force open the port. (Congress authorized him to raise 80,000 men for the campaign.) Though he was alarmed by the situation, Jefferson knew that time and America's restless and growing population were ultimately on his side.

In the end, luck was also on his side.

The confluence of two major historical events eventually convinced Napoleon to sell not just New Orleans but all of Louisiana to the Amer-icans: the catastrophic losses suffered by his army at the hands of black freedom fighters and malaria on the Caribbean island of San Domingo (later the independent nation of Haiti), and the resumption of war with Britain—a conflict that would require plenty of cash (as most wars do).

Napoleon decided to cut his losses in the Western Hemisphere and sell the territory for the sum of $15 million...approximately three cents per acre (approximately $230 million in today's dollars, or less than 42 cents per acre).

When news of the sale arrived in Washington, however, it stirred up political opposition not just from the Federalists, but from some members of Jefferson's party, because the deal was thought to be unconstitutional. Jefferson's own doubts about the legality of the transaction led him, initially, to pursue an amendment to the Constitution, as the 1787 Constitution contained no provisions for acquiring foreign territory. This move was consistent with Jefferson's attitude toward the federal government and presidential power, both of which he preferred to limit as much as possible.

It is one of history's great ironies, therefore, that he eventually ignored the lack of Constitutional authority. By doing so—by putting one vision above another—Jefferson set an early precedent for expanding the power of the presidency beyond the Constitution's explicit limits. By the time a special session of Congress was convened in October 1803, Jefferson had stopped talking about a Constitutional amendment and was instead applying his political muscle to getting the treaty ratified.

He didn't have to strain very hard.

After reports reached Washington that Napoleon was having second thoughts about the deal, and with the Spain threatening to ignore the treaty on the grounds that nobody knew the exact boundaries of Louisiana, Jefferson concluded that "the less that is said about my constitutional difficulty, the better; and that it will be desirable for Congress to do what is necessary *in silence*." If the choice was between sustaining his strict interpretation of executive authority or losing half a continent, he chose the more pragmatic course, all the while expressing the hope that "the good sense of our country will correct the evil of [broad] construction when it shall produce ill effects." Thanks to a huge majority of Republicans in Congress, the Louisiana purchase was easily ratified, as one senator put it, "in less time than required for the most trivial Indian contract."[13]

Another irony of the Louisiana Purchase is that while it reveals Jefferson's greatest strengths as a visionary, it also illuminates a key weakness. On the one hand, Jefferson demonstrated uncanny hindsight, sight, and foresight in recognizing the strategic and commercial value that the Louisiana Territory could provide to the nation that controlled it. Moreover, he revealed keen insight by moving deftly and decisively to acquire the land, despite reservations about the Constitutionality of the purchase. On the other hand, by brushing aside the Constitutional questions, Jefferson revealed one of his biggest flaws as a visionary—his tendency toward short-sighted foresight. On more than one occasion, he deliberately overlooked or dismissed some of the consequences that his visions might produce, brushing aside these objections by suggesting that future leaders (or the people) would do the right thing at some unspecified date in the future.

The most egregious example of this near-sighted foresight, from the point of view of the Democratic-Republicans, was the grand bargain Jefferson struck with Alexander Hamilton. In exchange for moving the nation's capital from Philadelphia to the new city of Washington, Jefferson (and Madison) conceded to Hamilton the federal government's right to assume the existing debts of the 13 states. In the near term, this was victory for Jefferson and his largely Southern-based party. In the long term, however, it was a political blunder of the first magnitude for a party that championed states' rights and a weak central government. By assuming the states' debts, Treasury Secretary Hamilton deftly transferred the financial interests (and allegiance) of thousands of disparate bond owners from the state capitals to the Treasury Department in Washington, helping him build a loyal constituency of industrialists, bankers, attorneys, and stock speculators whose fortunes depended on what the federal government did.

While his tendency to think short-term doesn't nullify Jefferson's genius as an inspirational visionary, it *does* reflect the importance of assessing how your vision is executed, so the results of the realized vision will maximize *positive* and *intentional* consequences and minimize any undesirable side effects. (For more about *execution*, see Chapter 4.)

Jefferson possessed the four essential qualities of vision: hindsight, sight, foresight, and insight—and these qualities made all the difference in his ability to advance his vision. As a leader, you must constantly work to develop these essential qualities to take your organization or your family to new and exciting places.

A NEW GENERATION CRAVES VISION

As a leader, you must communicate a compelling vision, and make sure that vision is spread throughout the organization so it will generate significant results. The realization of "what could be" is the picture that must be painted—not just earnings, not just the bottom line. Yes, you do have to focus and talk about the bottom line, or your organization will die. But that is where the insight factor comes in. You must have keen insight into the culture and people's mindsets.

Today, I see a whole generation of young people who are entering the workforce, people who want significance in their lives. They are saying, "Yes, my dad graduated college and went straight to work for Halliburton or IBM, but I want to spend a year in Haiti digging wells. Then I'll come back and work for the rest of my life." As Stephen Colbert recently put it, the younger generation wants something more than "working 80 hours a week and then coming home to weep silently over their sleeping children."

What is true in the workforce is also true in the home. I think families should also develop a vision for what they want to accomplish—for the direction they want to go as a family, the things they want to do as a family. Why should only companies have a vision for the future? Why should everybody else just float along? I think it's the responsibility of parents, not to dictate a vision to their children, but to vision-cast on behalf of their children—to show and teach their children how to build dreams and visions.

This type of vision-casting is desperately needed in our culture today.

When I grew up (and perhaps when you did, too) kids went out on summer mornings and played all day. They came home for lunch and then went back out and played until dark. That's how life was. Kids went out and picked up a stick and the stick became a sword and they whacked their friends over the head with the sticks. That's what boys do. I used to run around with the lid from a metal garbage can; it was my shield. Since we lived in Miami, we also threw key limes at each other. That was what we did.

What do children do today? They sit on the couch and play video games. Kids today aren't challenged with the task of thinking creatively—if only to avoid sheer boredom, because they're not being challenged and tasked to think creatively. Visions and possibilities are created *for them* by the people who produce video games and television programs, and they simply choose among the different pre-set options.

Recently, we had a children's choir from Africa come to my church to sing. And when I say they "sang," I mean they beat drums and danced with a relish and enthusiasm you rarely see these days among American children. What do we do with kids in many American churches? We demand that they stand up straight, don't move, sing on cue, and look bored out of their minds. The kids from Africa were living it up. They had smiles on their faces. They were having a blast.

We have squelched creativity so much in our culture that I believe it's squelching our children's ability to vision-cast, to think about the unseen possibilities and pathways for their lives. We must ask our children, teenagers, and young adults, "What do you want to do with your life?" and not just, "How do you want to make money?" As parents, we have to help our kids develop the ability to dream beyond the mundane, or they will starve—not physically, but emotionally, mentally, and creatively.

It's time to paint compelling visions for what your children could become.

Don't give up on your vision. Sometimes visions take more time to fulfill than we ever imagined. That is one of the hardest and most important lessons I've learned about leadership. Timing is not always controlled by a clock, and our critics will often scoff at the delays. But when the vision finally comes to fruition, what a great sense of accomplishment you will enjoy!

I keep this quote from Joseph Ellis by my desk, and it never fails to inspire me: "Grand visions, even ones that prove as prescient as Washington's, must nevertheless negotiate the damnable particularities that history in the short run tosses up before history in the long run arrives to validate the vision."[14]

Don't give up on your vision. One day, history will validate your foresight, insight, and endurance.

> *"Both the hummingbird and the vulture fly over our nation's deserts. All vultures see is rotting meat, because that is what they look for. They thrive on that diet. But hummingbirds ignore the smelly flesh of dead animals. Instead, they look for the colorful blossoms of desert plants. The vultures live on what was. They live on the past. They fill themselves with what is dead and gone. But hummingbirds live on what is. They seek new life. They fill themselves with freshness and life. Each bird finds what it is looking for. We all do."[15]*
>
> —Steve Goodier

CHAPTER THREE

GEORGE WASHINGTON: THE ART OF INFLUENCE

When the best leader's work is done, the people say,
"We did it ourselves."
—Lao Tzu

GEORGE WASHINGTON MANAGED to accomplish nothing less than fathering a fledgling nation toward greatness. From the Battle of Long Island to the British surrender at Yorktown and the presidency, Washington led Americans through war, victory, and the formation of a national government, enabling us to spread our wings and fly. He established many of our guiding principles, setting precedents we still follow more than 200 years later.

Born February 22, 1732, George entered the family of Augustine and Mary Washington, an ambitious couple who continually migrated toward new opportunities. Though little is known about his childhood, we know that George was taught the value of hard work, honesty, and good character.

As an adult, he inherited the plantation known as Mount Vernon and worked as a surveyor in the Ohio Valley, which served him well in the military. At age 21, he was thrust onto the world stage, thanks to his role in an incident that, historians believe, ignited the French and Indian War. While serving as a major in the Virginia militia, Washington led an ambush against a "hostile" French army unit—a unit that may actually have been on a peaceful diplomatic mission. This action led to the murder of a French officer, an accusation of assassination against George Washington, and the start of the French and Indian War.

In the years that followed, Washington returned to private life at Mount Vernon, but eventually the escalating conflict between crown and colonies goaded him from the sidelines. After he was appointed head of the Continental Army in 1776, he led the colonies through eight years of war to independence. Following Cornwallis' surrender at Yorktown, Washington turned his attention to birthing the new nation. He took part in the Constitutional Convention and thereafter served as our first President, recognizing that everything he did and said would set the standard for succeeding generations.

More than just the stoic face on the one-dollar bill, Washington was the face of the nation. For several generations, in fact, Washington was *literally* the face of the Presidency. If you study a photograph of the Ford's Theater booth in which Lincoln was shot, for example, you'll notice a framed photograph of George Washington. At the time, the presidency had no official seal, so a portrait of George Washington was used to symbolize the presidency.

COMMAND AND CONTROL VERSUS INFLUENCE

Washington's career illustrates the two main ways in which leaders galvanize followers to realize a vision: through command and control and through influence.

A good leader uses both.

A good leader exerts command and control when necessary, but uses influence at all times. The difference between the two methods is that influence stems from love—from a genuine concern and care for individuals or a cause. Influence stirs the soul. Command and control, on the other hand, leverages the fear of punishments and the promise of rewards.

I can't inspire my dog to do anything. I can only command him to do things. Because people aren't dogs, good leadership depends as much on the ability to inspire as to control—the ability to touch the souls of followers and light a fire that will drive them to overcome any obstacles in their path.

For most of the 20th century, however, most business leaders looked not to George Washington as an "influence leader" role model, but to Frederick Taylor, whose book *The Principles of Scientific Management* was published in 1911. Taylor pioneered the concept of dividing organizations into "thinking people" (managers) and "executing people" (workers). He regarded managers as *thinking leaders*, whose job was to direct the non-thinking human resources. Taylor's principles are premised on the notion that people dislike work and will avoid it whenever possible. Hence, they must be induced to work through a combination of threats and bribery, because they are motivated mainly by money and the fear of losing their jobs. Because most workers would rather follow commands than accept responsibility for decision-making, most of them will display very little creativity on the job, except when it comes to shirking responsibility and finding clever ways to avoid the rules.[16]

Washington would have been appalled by this philosophy. Though he was intimately familiar with human frailty and foibles, his leadership reflected a belief that people could be inspired to perform miracles—if only the leader created the right conditions. People could be influenced and motivated. They could be encouraged not just to *accept* responsibility for their decisions, but persuaded to actively *pursue* that responsibility.

Far from treating his officers and men as chess pieces to be maneuvered across a giant board, Washington relied on their creativity and ingenuity. He solicited ideas, feedback, and advice from subordinates at every possible opportunity. During his war councils (committees he convened before a major military action), Washington not only solicited feedback from his junior officers, he even allowed them to overrule his own plans. On more than one occasion, Washington's subordinates persuaded him to cancel operations that, in their view, would have ended in disaster.

Washington understood that influence and inspiration can light new fires and rekindle dying embers. He was often called upon to rekindle the flame of patriotic fervor and determination in the men, fanning their enthusiasm, uplifting their flagging spirits, and encouraging them to persevere against seemingly hopeless odds.

During the war, Washington had to overcome short-term enlistments, desertions, poorly clad and equipped soldiers, an inefficient

Congress, and wavering loyalty among the population. Still, enough soldiers and civilians trusted him that they stayed with the cause.

With the advantage of hindsight, we Americans tend to regard the war's outcome as something preordained by Heaven. Not true. Throughout the war, ultimate victory was very much in doubt. This was especially true during the final two months of 1776, probably the darkest days of the Revolution. Following the Continental Army's defeat at the Battle of Long Island (now Brooklyn) and the evacuation of Manhattan, Washington's army fled across New Jersey—an inglorious retreat that produced widespread depression among the soldiers and citizenry. As Washington simultaneously retreated and begged for reinforcements from his subordinate Charles Lee, Lee was plotting for the overthrow of his chief, whispering slanders, and writing to governors of states and members of Congress, asserting that the recent disasters were caused by Washington's incompetency, and that it would all have turned out differently if his advice had been heeded. To Dr. Rush of Philadelphia, Lee declared in substance that he could bring order out of chaos if he were made dictator for one week.

As half the army was fleeing like hunted foxes across the Jersey plains, with men departing for their homes by the hundreds, believing the cause to be a lost one, the other half was held inactive by a traitor a hundred miles away.

Furthermore, the gloomy outlook had led some 3000 of the leading Jersey farmers to accept British General Howe's latest offer and to swear allegiance to the Crown. The patriot cause had now reached its lowest ebb. Howe believed that armed resistance had collapsed, and he retired to New York, while Cornwallis prepared to board a ship for England. New Jersey was held in the firm grasp of the British.

But the dawn was beginning to break upon the darkness. The volunteers from Philadelphia arrived in camp, Sullivan came with the troops that Lee had held so long, and Horatio Gates joined the army with 2000 men, sent from the upper Hudson. Washington now determined on a bold stroke. He would re-cross the Delaware by night and attack the Hessians at Trenton.[17]

Catching the enemy wholly unprepared, the Americans scored a crushing victory at Trenton.

After the battle, though, many of Washington's soldiers were preparing to leave because their enlistments were up. Washington urgently appealed to them to step forward and stay with him to fight for their noble cause. Reluctantly at first, but then by the hundreds, the soldiers stepped forward to re-enlist. There was something about the man, George Washington, that caused these men to give up the things they loved dearly for a cause they believed was worthy of their utmost devotion. It was in *that moment* that George Washington saved both the Continental Army and the revolutionary cause.

I can think of no better example of *influential leadership* in action.

—

Many leaders are driven by the power of command and control, but they don't consider whether this style of leadership is sustainable. In my experience, inspirational/influential leadership is indefinitely sustainable, whereas command and control is not, especially when you need your people to persevere in the face of difficult or dangerous odds. In those instances, systems of reward and punishment are of limited value. In most cases, soft power is usually more effective than hard power.

When Steve Jobs was driving Apple, it's clear he was a command-and-control leader—a hands-on, in-your-face kind of person. Yes, he had the ability to inspire employees and colleagues, but the way he led the organization was tilted toward command and control. As a recent review of *Inside Apple* noted: "In the wake of Jobs' death, more of Apple's business methods are coming to light—and they're the polar opposite of what you'd learn in management school. Contrary to current business trends toward transparency and flatter hierarchies, Apple has fiercely encouraged secretiveness, silos, and a start-up mentality, even though it is the most profitable company on Earth...By the time [the author is] finished, you'll probably still want to buy Apple products, but you may not want to work for the firm."

Conversely, people who knew former Dallas Cowboys' coach Tom Landry have all said the same thing: They would have run through a brick wall if he'd asked them. Landry inspired people. He inspired them with his quietness, his caring, and his determination. He would get in someone's face to make a point if need be, but he also exercised a higher degree of influence than most coaches because he demonstrated that he cared about his people. I've heard countless stories from people who said, "Tom Landry was concerned first and foremost about me as a person and second as a football player."

Hall of Famer Mike Ditka says Tom Landry was one of the most influential people in his life. "I decided to retire from football. I get a phone call on December 28. I answer the phone and he says, 'Mike, this is Tom Landry with the Dallas Cowboys. I don't know if you can play football anymore or not, but I just traded for you.' Well that wasn't very inspirational, but he said, 'I'm willing to take a chance on you if you'll take a chance on yourself.' Tom Landry is the reason I'm sitting here... He changed the way I thought about a lot of things, football and other things. If he wouldn't have come into my life when he did, I'd probably be tending bar somewhere in Pittsburgh."[18]

The boss who inspires and influences stands in the front lines.

Command-and-control people tend to stand in the back. The "carrot leader" works from the front: "Follow me!"

The "whip leader" sits in the back of the boat barking orders: "Row, row, row!"

In December 1777, Washington faced circumstances just as dire as those before Trenton, leading ill-fed, poorly equipped soldiers to winter camp at Valley Forge. Although Horatio Gates and Benedict Arnold had won a stunning victory at Saratoga in September, Washington had lost the capital of Philadelphia. The French had yet to enter the war, and a smallpox epidemic soon ravaged the weak and weary troops.

Even as food and clothing were gathered and shelters built, Washington and his officers drilled the men into shape with the aid of Baron von Steuben. Day after day, the men were trained in military tactics and discipline. Washington also inspired the soldiers by having them read the Revolutionary pamphlets of Thomas Paine, who'd recently written, "The harder the conflict, the more glorious the triumph."[19] Washington had to balance hard power and soft power to inspire men in times when the triumph didn't seem possible, much less glorious.

Hard power is supported by implicit or explicit promises of reward and punishment. Influence is a form of soft power that requires that you *persuade*—not force—your team to perform the arduous tasks. Whether you persuade them by appealing to their altruism or motivated self-interest, you inspire your people to become self-motivated. That's what Washington did. Sometimes he had to stand behind his men, threatening to shoot anyone who retreated, but most of the time he inspired them to charge into the fury of musket balls and cannon fire. Conversely, the average British soldier didn't want to be in America. His only motivation was pay and fear of the extreme penalties for insubordination and desertion.

Inspiration summons people to achieve greater things than they would on their own. It calls upon the better angels of our nature. At the same time, it helps people grow as persons and professionals.

I'm not suggesting that command and control should be abandoned. It has its place. However, the leader must know when to exercise hard power or soft power. Sometimes you've got to "love your kids toward the right things," and sometimes you've got to "forcefully inspire" them in the right direction. Like a great coach, Washington motivated his men to do things they normally wouldn't have done. There were times when influence was not enough, however, and he had to use the command and control that came with his position to force the men in line. At times, he had to mete out discipline and punishment, including execution of deserters. Washington may have been influential and inspirational, but he wasn't magic.

Soft power is sometimes confused with weakness. It's not weakness—it is strength under control. Soft power is expressed subtly over extended periods of time, rather than exploding in short, sometimes brutal, bursts.

Ultimately, a leader either understands the value of soft power or doesn't. I won't convince someone with an authoritarian mindset that inspiration is as valuable a tool as control and coercion. The more cynical people I've met tend to have an authoritarian mindset to feed their insecurities. Unfortunately, most of these people tend to be motivated mainly by money, titles, and power, rather than visions of how to improve the lives of customers, consumers, and communities.

*"The key to successful leadership today
is influence, not authority."*

—Ken Blanchard

LEADERSHIP BY EXAMPLE

Do not underestimate the power of influencing by example. Washington influenced through personal example so many times and in so many ways that the stories have filled many a book. As a boy, he was so determined to improve himself that he hand-copied the *Rules of Civility & Decent Behavior*, a Jesuit guide to gentlemanly conduct. These rules guided his conduct for the remainder of his life. Although some of the guidelines seem ridiculous by today's standards ("Put not off your Cloths in the presence of Others") or antiquated ("Spit not in the Fire, nor Stoop low before it"), many stressed what today we call people skills, including body language and active listening.

- Every Action done in Company, ought to be with Some Sign of Respect, to those that are Present.

- Sleep not when others Speak, Sit not when others stand, Speak not when you Should hold your Peace, walk not on when others Stop.

- Be no Flatterer, neither Play with any that delights not to be Play'd Withal.

- The Gestures of the Body must be Suited to the discourse you are upon.

- Reproach none for the Infirmities of Nature, nor Delight to Put them that have in mind thereof.

- Show not yourself glad at the Misfortune of another though he were your enemy.

- When you see a Crime punished, you may be inwardly Pleased; but always show Pity to the Suffering Offender.[20]

Washington chose as role models some of the most virtuous men of the ancient world, including the Roman statesman Cato. He was especially fond of a play about Cincinnatus, the Roman farmer who left his plough to lead an army that saved Rome, whereupon he refused the role of dictator when it was offered by the Senate. (Sound familiar?)

From a young age, Washington sought military fame and displayed unparalleled courage. It's a miracle he wasn't maimed or killed, considering how many times he charged through storms of shot and shell. His first experience with this occurred in June 1755 during the French and Indian War. While marching through the Alleghenies with an army commanded by General Edward Braddock, Washington recommended that a lightly equipped column advance from the main column to Fort Duquesne (what is today Pittsburgh). The next day, disaster struck. The French and their Indian allies ambushed this vanguard of troops. In the massacre that ensued, hundreds of British and American soldiers, including General Braddock, fell to both enemy *and* friendly fire.

With Braddock and his aides dead or wounded, Washington charged into the midst of the slaughter to rally the remaining soldiers. "Riding back and forth amidst the chaos, two horses were shot out beneath him and four musket balls pierced his coat, but he miraculously escaped without a scratch."[21] Whether he was bolstering his reputation for bravery or actually meant it, Washington famously wrote his brother, "I heard the bullets whistle, and, believe me, there is something charming in the sound."

Perhaps he meant a bullet going *by* was charming. Or perhaps he really *did* like the sound of gunfire in the morning, for he was to race into the middle of withering fire time and again during the Revolutionary War, despite pleas from his aides not to risk his life. At Monmouth, New Jersey in 1778, American troops were in retreat and disarray when Washington took personal control. Lafayette said "his presence stopped the retreat." Alexander Hamilton wrote, "Other officers have great merit in performing their parts well, but he directed the whole with the skill of a master workman...I never saw the General to so much advantage." The British retreated to New York.

It should be noted that aside from a single sojourn to Mount Vernon, Washington stayed with his troops in the field throughout the war. Furthermore, he never accepted any pay for his services (other than reimbursement for expenses). (Later, during the Whiskey Rebellion, Washington also became the only sitting president in history to personally lead troops into armed conflict, leading 15,000 troops into Pennsylvania on horseback.)

Perhaps the greatest test of Washington's influence and powers of persuasion occurred not on the battlefield, but after the British defeat at Yorktown. In March 1783, a conspiracy was hatched by a group of congressmen and some of Washington's officers, including Henry Knox and Horatio Gates. Originally, the plan was to threaten a military coup to assure passage of certain revenue-raising legislation, but a split developed among the officers. Gates' faction was prepared to seize control of the national government. The crisis reached a head on March 11, when the officers scheduled a meeting to coordinate strategy. Washington countermanded the order, and scheduled another meeting for March 16.

In the hours before the meeting, Washington struggled to write a speech that would dissuade his unhappy officers from pursuing this disastrous course—a course that has destroyed many a republic before and since. The dream of American democracy was something personal to

Washington—very personal. He made that clear in his speech, telling the men that he would view a betrayal of the Revolution's ideals as a personal affront.

According to legend, Washington won his officers' hearts without saying a word. Setting his notes aside, he paused and, reaching into his pocket, he produced a pair of reading glasses. "Gentlemen, you will permit me to put on my spectacles," he declared, "for I have not only grown gray but almost blind in service to my country."[22] Within seconds, there wasn't a dry eye in the room. The conspiracy was quelled right then and there.

Like his hero Cincinnatus, Washington refused the mantle of a Caesar when it was offered to him. Upon learning that Washington intended to reject the mantle of emperor, George III (his archenemy nonetheless) is alleged to have said, "If he does that, he will be the greatest man in the world."[23]

I've known plenty of leaders who say, "This is what we need to do." Then they step back or walk away. They don't participate in the actual effort. Obviously, this causes the people down in the trenches to look back and think, "How committed *is* this person to achieving the vision?"

The command-and-control leader tends to stand back and watch everybody do the work. Like Washington, the influence-and-inspire leader gets his hands dirty. He recognizes that inspiring people means getting personally involved—getting connected and literally becoming part of the team effort. Real leadership is not sitting in the ivory tower or corner office barking orders to subordinates. Real leadership is demonstrated in the trenches, with the people.

History is fraught with examples of leaders who were not where they should have been when it all broke loose. In the Bible, the story of David and Bathsheba centers around the fact that David's armies and his troops were involved in a war. The Bible says it was the time of year when kings go off to war, but David didn't go. He stayed back and looked out his window, and saw Bathsheba. The next thing you know, he's got a baby on his hands. Leadership means being where you are supposed to be—out in front, leading people where they need to go.

REPUTATION MATTERS

Well before the last Founding Father left this Earth, Americans were lamenting the twilight of a Golden Era and comparing their current leaders unfavorably with the visionary titans of Washington, Jefferson, Adams, Franklin, and their peers. To this day, most of us are awestruck that such an assemblage of intellectual and altruistic giants appeared from nowhere to defeat the world's most powerful military machine and lay the foundations of a mighty republic. Sometimes wistfully, sometimes bitterly, we wonder why the nation has never again been blessed with men like the Founders—why our current leaders seem like dwarfs standing on the shoulders of the gods.

Though this attitude is largely steeped in nostalgia, there are genuine differences to be found in characters of the Revolutionary leaders and many leaders today. One of them is the importance that the Founders attached to their reputations. Compared with most contemporary business, political, and religious leaders in America, the Founders were positively obsessed with their reputations—to an extent that often seems nonsensical. And no leader was more zealous about building and guarding his reputation than George Washington. To Washington and his contemporaries, reputation was no mere matter of ego and status. It was a matter of honor, and honor was everything. These men were keenly aware that they would be role models for future generations, and they wanted posterity not just to think well of them but to emulate their virtuous deeds. Okay, there was a certain amount of ego involved, but in their minds, the future of the nation also depended on the "brands" that they cultivated for themselves.

Many of Washington's actions after 1783 can be understood only in terms of this deep concern for his reputation as a virtuous leader. He was constantly on guard and very sensitive to any criticism. Jefferson said that no one was more sensitive. Washington judged all his actions by what people might think of them. This sometimes makes him seem silly to modern minds, but not to those of the 18th century. In that very suspicious age in which people were acutely "jealous" of what great men were up to, Washington thought it important that people understand his motives. The reality was not enough; he had to appear virtuous. He was obsessed that he not seem base, mean, avaricious, or unduly ambitious. No one, said Jefferson, worked harder than Washington in keeping "motives of interest or consanguinity, of friendship or hatred" from influencing him. He had a lifelong preoccupation with his reputation for "disinterestedness."[24]

In 1783, Washington agreed to become the first president of the newly formed Order of the Cincinnati, a fraternity of retired revolutionary army officers. However, when a public outcry was raised against the group because of its "aristocratic" nature, he pleaded with friends for advice. At Jefferson's suggestion, Washington put pressure on the group to reform its rules, especially the rule that made membership in the society hereditary. After all, the leader of a new democratic society could not appear to be leading a gang of self-styled noblemen.

Once again, during the winter of 1784-85, Washington's reputation was put on the spot. The Virginia Assembly presented him with shares in the James River and Potomac canal companies to honor his service to the nation and the cause of canal building. On the one hand, he believed the shares might look like a pay-off, compromising his reputation for virtue. On the other hand, he was a big believer in what we would today call government-sponsored infrastructure projects, and he didn't want to show disrespect to a cause in which he truly believed. To break this ethical deadlock, Washington devoted months to agonizing over a decision, writing to everyone he knew to solicit their advice.

The story would be almost comical if Washington had not been so deadly earnest. He certainly understated the situation when he told his correspondents that his mind was "not a little agitated" by the problem. In letter after letter he expressed real anguish. This was no ordinary display of scruples such as government officials today show over a conflict of interest; in 1784 and 1785 Washington was not even holding public office.

Once again Jefferson found the key to Washington's anxieties and told him that declining to accept the shares would only add to his reputation for disinterestedness. So Washington gave them away to the college that eventually became Washington and Lee.[25] It's fascinating to examine the concern of the Founding Fathers—and Washington in particular—with what posterity would think. "What will people think about me?" is a question that more leaders today should ask themselves, because reputation is still a major factor in winning hearts and minds. Had it not been for Washington's awesome reputation, the precedents he set as president would have meant little or nothing. It was reputation alone, and the respect succeeding presidents showed for it, that prompted them to follow his leadership during and after his lifetime. Until the mid-20th century, for example, there was no Constitutional limit on the number of terms a president could seek. Until 1940, however, no president sought more than two terms simply because the nation's first president had declined a third term. *That* is soft power. That is influence through reputation. Nothing stopped anyone from seeking three terms, but for nearly 150 years, no president dared because none of them dared break with the precedent Washington had set in 1796 in refusing a third term. (The phrase "so help me God" spoken at the end of the Presidential Oath of Office was also a Washington precedent, as was the president's "cabinet" of advisors.)

It is telling that, in terms of their reputations, the Founders were thinking about the long-term and not just the short-term, "What are people saying about me today?"

It's also of note that Washington wore his uniform when he visited the Continental Congress following Lexington and Concord. He showed up in dress uniform when nobody else did, even though he had long since retired from the military. There is no doubt that this greatly influenced Congress' decision to appoint him commander-in-chief. When they were debating who would lead the army, and there's one guy sitting in a military uniform...well, that's like asking "Which one do we send to Disney World? How about the guy wearing the Mickey Mouse ears?"

This event most clearly reveals the intersection of reputation and influence.

THE INFLUENCE LEADER RISES ABOVE DEFEAT

How can a leader keep people motivated following setbacks and failures? By recasting and restating the ultimate vision.

Individual methods and strategies don't always work. Because of this, you must sometimes recast the bigger picture and reinforce the big vision. Washington lost plenty of battles during the Revolution, but he kept coming back. He kept motivating his men by reminding them of the ultimate goal—to win the war and their independence. You have to continue to provide clarity about the results you're trying to achieve in order to drive people forward, to help everyone stay emotionally connected to the success of the cause.

History is written by the winners. That adage is true to a certain extent, yet it is surprising how many figures in history experienced the depths of defeat even more often than victory. Abraham Lincoln lost more elections than he won, and George Washington was no stranger to defeat—in fact, he probably saw more defeats than victories in his military career. He learned, however, how to rise above the loss and live to fight another day.

Most of that famed year, 1776, consisted of one loss after another. The final blow was the tremendous loss of New York to the British. By the end of that year, Washington had lost parts of three states, and 90 percent of the army under his command.[26] But he continued to rise above the defeats and lead his men to the next battle...and the next. Washington knew that if the leader was defeated, the army would never rise to fight again. As in most organizations, the colonial army was not going to rise above its leader. Washington knew how critical it was for him to find the inner fortitude needed to prevent a single defeat from becoming a final defeat.

That does not mean Washington was immune to the pain of loss. For all his great character strengths, the general was a man of great pride. A loss was a loss, and great generals are not fans of failure. However, Washington had mastered himself. He knew that controlling his emotions in the midst of defeat was paramount. As the great Washington biographer Douglas Southall Freeman wrote, Washington could war better against the British "because he was not at war with himself."[27]

Washington's character became the governor of his emotions, and this was critical to his stewardship of the American Revolution. One of Washington's great strengths of character was his ability to command not only men, but even more problematic, his emotions. He rarely allowed himself to show discouragement to his men, but his writings reveal that this was a constant battle.

November 16, 1776, would be a day of sadness and defeat for Washington. The place was Fort Washington in the Harlem Heights section of New York. Washington, through the recommendation of some trusted advisors, decided to leave the garrison to attack British troops who were pushing through Manhattan. He knew the enemy must be stopped from marching to Philadelphia and taking the capital, so he divided his army, setting one force against the advancing British and leaving the other to garrison the fort—even though some of his officers thought the garrison would be "sitting ducks." Washington believed the British commander, General Howe, would not attack the fort but would put the fort to siege. The men in the fort, Washington believed, would have plenty of time to evacuate.

Washington underestimated the enemy. The British viewed the fort as an easy take and proceeded to march against it. Washington moved with some men toward Philadelphia, then heard of the British advance on the fort and hurried back. It was too little, too late. As the British attacked, the choice was simple: be annihilated or surrender. After the loss of many lives, the decision to surrender was unavoidable. It was the worst defeat to date for the Continental Army. Washington lost some 3,000 men, several pieces of artillery, and much of his reputation for leadership. Criticism of his ability to lead the army was at an all-time high, with some of the greatest wounds coming from people he considered his close friends.

Washington cried like a baby, grieving over the loss of life and the futures of the men headed to the grisly conditions aboard British prison ships. As the commander-in-chief, he knew he had to control his emotions to accomplish the greater good—to prevent his feelings from becoming contagious and dispiriting the men even more.

Refusing to publicly reveal his despair, Washington reached deep within his reserves of strength and found the ability to overcome this blow to the cause of independence.

Some people like to say that "failure is not an option." Well, sometimes failure happens, regardless of whether you considered it an option. It happens, and when it does, you must decide whether the failure means "time to restart" or "time to admit total defeat."

DON'T TRY TO COVER UP FAILURES AND MISTAKES

One of the biggest mistakes leaders make when attempting to influence people is dismissing or denying failures and mistakes. To deny mistakes and failures is to patronize your team members—to treat them like fools. They *know* mistakes have been made, and who made them. The same advice applies to minimizing those mistakes or failures. "Oh well, it'll be all right. Don't worry about it." Telling people things are not as severe as they seem, or that a particular setback doesn't matter will compound the damage that's been done. Worse, your credibility as a leader (and an intelligent human being) may well suffer.

I'd rather hear the boss admit, "We blew it—it didn't work out" than, "Nothing to worry about." I'd be glad to hear an admission rather than some crisis communication double-talk. Chances are, I know the situation is bad. I know things didn't work out. In my experience, most teams will appreciate such candor. Unfortunately, many leaders fear that they'll be viewed as weak or incompetent if they admit to failure. Granted, if you fail big enough your board of directors may fire you, but honesty is always the best policy.

Give people room to fail. If your people don't fail occasionally, they're probably not trying very hard. In fact, they're probably not trying at all. They're certainly not trying to achieve big things.

Of course, when encouraging people to rise above failure, it helps if the leader is somewhat articulate—well-spoken enough to inspire. However, you don't have to be a master orator or rhetorician to accomplish this goal. You merely need to be clear and articulate enough to explain what you've done, what you're doing now, where you are going, and why it matters. If you can't communicate that, you have a problem. In general, however, the content of your communication is more important than rhetorical bells and whistles. We can't all be Thomas Paine (as we will see in Chapter 6).

Yogi Berra was a magnificent leader of the New York Yankees during the 1950s, despite his penchant for statements such as "Ninety percent of this game is half mental." He wasn't especially eloquent, but he was frequently wise. More important, he was uniquely persuasive because he said things from the heart, and that endeared him to many people. You may not be William Shakespeare or Yogi Berra, but you need to understand the importance of good communication, especially in times of failure.

When faced with failure, it's important to be aware of, and then communicate, the obstacles you are facing. From there, recast the vision and how that vision (modified, if need be) will help you overcome those unforeseen obstacles. Emphasize how the grand vision is greater and more powerful than any obstacle you could confront.

And like Washington, always keep your chin up—at least in front of the "troops." If you don't keep your chin up, you won't see where you're going. Nobody likes to follow a leader who's down in the mouth. Nobody wants to follows a leader whose head is hung low.

I was recently talking with a friend who had been speaking at an event. In the line-up just before him was Dick Burleson, a former head of college football referees. Burleson has written a book called *You Better Be Right*. In his speech, Dick said, "I don't fear 100 lions led by a sheep. I fear 100 sheep led by a lion." He was challenging the audience to be a lion. A leader who can really inspire people can take 100 sheep and do amazing things with them.

One of the most intriguing praises of Washington comes from the oft-forgotten Founding Father Gouverneur Morris, the author of much of the preamble of the Constitution. He said Washington had the unique ability to master the inner passions that raged within him.

He noted that Washington was a man of great passion, which had the capacity to boil over into a rage. Many an officer and enlisted man were objects of that near-rage passion. However, Washington also had the ability to tame those passions, and demonstrate a level of self-control that let him lead with a fiery passion that didn't burn those around him. Instead, he inspired and influenced those around him to achieve things greater than they ever thought possible.

The famed portrait artist Gilbert Stuart said of the general, "Had he been born in the forests, he would have been the fiercest man among the savage tribes."[28] Washington's ability to keep those passions bridled enabled him to lead with ferocity, passion, and focus. And yet he did so with the serenity and the calm required of all great leaders. Inspiration is fiery passion under control, and it is essential to accomplishing the vision.

CHAPTER FOUR

JOHN ADAMS: UNSHAKEABLE CONVICTION

T HE CHARM OF THE MOVIE *Forrest Gump* stems not just from the title character's lovable demeanor or simple-minded-yet-profound statements, but the fact that Forrest always found himself at the center of history. Whether greeting President Kennedy, meeting Elvis Presley, or inspiring the "Have a Nice Day" smiley face symbol, Gump was serendipitously at the center of pop culture and history. Gump came to symbolize many of the Baby Boomer generation who blindly stumbled through the historical moments of their lives.

If there is one man of the Revolution who was always at the center of events, and always aware of their significance, it was John Adams.

Short, frumpy, and often fractious, Adams was present at every moment of the new nation's birth and adolescence. Even when serving his country from overseas, his heart never left his beloved Massachusetts or the nation he believed could change the world. Although he wasn't a "people person" like Franklin, a wordsmith like Jefferson, or a soldier like Washington, Adams was a man of tremendous vision and conviction. He was convinced that America could realize an awesome destiny if it would follow the paths he charted.

Adams, though one of my personal favorites, is not one of the most popular Founding Fathers, but if not for his prescience and determination, the Revolution might have ended very differently. Adams was instrumental in formulating the Massachusetts constitution, a document that would lay the groundwork for many other constitutions, including that of the United States. It was Adams who led the call for a Continental Congress. It was Adams who nominated Washington to lead the army (much to the chagrin of fellow Bostonian John Hancock, who desperately wanted the job and believed he was the best man for the position). Adams was the one who nominated Jefferson to pen the Declaration of Independence, and it was Adams who helped obtain foreign investments to fund the war.

Born in 1735 to John, Sr. and Susanna Boylston, Adams was raised on the farm and in the church. He was educated at Harvard, and his father fully expected him to become a minister, but Adams had other plans. His rise to fame was steady, but not meteoric. Though he was filled with passion and zeal, his articulation of those passions wasn't voiced as loudly or intensely as that of his cousin Samuel Adams (see Chapter 6). Instead, John chose to express himself through his legal work, his writing, and his commitment to principle.

From his defense of the British soldiers involved in the Boston Massacre to the Continental Congress, to the formulation of the Treaty of Paris that would end the Revolutionary War, to the Constitutional Convention, the vice presidency, and ultimately the presidency, Adams was a vital part of the nation's formation. Had he never been born, the cause of independence might have taken many more years to win popular support.

Adams was notoriously temperamental and moody, and often felt alone and irrelevant. But if there was anyone during this period who was not irrelevant, it was Adams. He was, however, constantly frustrated by what he deemed a lack of respect toward him, and he was prone to fits of depression. Always eager to voice his opinion, he sometimes did so to his own detriment. As Jay Winik has noted, Adams was a gadfly—a role he didn't have to play.[29]

Benjamin Franklin summarized Adams' character best when he said Adams was a man who "means well for his Country, is always an honest Man, often a Wise One, but sometimes and in some things, absolutely out of his senses."[30]

His saving grace was his wife Abigail. Perhaps no other woman at the nation's founding was more influential and cognizant of her supporting role. She was a partner and an equal. She furthered Adams' sense of right, and raised the spirits of her "dearest friend" at critical points. "I can do nothing without you," he would remind her frequently.[31] Marrying Abigail was Adams' most important decision personally. Politically, she helped fortify the sense of justice that was already bred into him by his parents and the Congregational Church.

(The bond and partnership between the two was well-portrayed in the HBO miniseries based on the Pulitzer-prize-winning book *John Adams* by David McCullough. It was broadcast in 2008 and won four Golden Globe awards and 13 Emmys, more than any other miniseries in history.)

For all his faults, Adams was a man of principle. Combined with conviction, passion, and his spiritual grounding, this made him a model for future generations—a model of the type of courage needed to realize important and lasting goals.

WHAT IS A "WORTHY" CAUSE?

Few people ever commit to anything as passionately, and for such a sustained period, as John Adams committed to the cause of liberty. The reason is quite simple: Only those goals we deem "worthy" will compel us to persevere against every impediment and obstacle.

You may have met people who seem to "commit" to a particular cause one day, and shift gears the next...and again the next. You may have met people who change their visions as often as they change their socks. Obviously, this isn't a genuine commitment. This behavior reflects someone in *search* of a commitment. What such people lack is not willingness to commit, but deep-seated conviction—an intuitive "knowing" that they absolutely must follow a particular course and champion a particular vision. To truly commit, you must absolutely know that you cannot stop until the dream is fulfilled. There is no stopping. There is no going back. There is no room for ultimate failure, though there may be setbacks en route. As George W. Bush said in his speech to the nation following the attacks of 9/11, "We will not tire, we will not falter, and we will not fail." That's the degree of conviction needed to commit to a vision...and stay committed. Unfortunately, there's no quick questionnaire or litmus test to help determine whether a vision is worth the sacrifice of time, energy, and emotion. We may judge some causes worthy because they've tugged at our heartstrings—e.g., raising money for breast cancer research because a loved one died of the disease. We may decide that a cause is worthwhile because it will enhance our status or boost our ego—e.g., scaling the tallest mountain on every continent. Or we may find a cause compelling because our "gut" tells us that *this* is the way. Whatever the reason, deciding to commit to a cause greater than ourselves is an intensely personal—if not always altruistic—process, especially when the stakes are as high as those John Adams was willing to risk: his life, his fortune, and his "sacred honor."

What would prompt Adams and the other Founding Fathers to gamble their property, their honor, and their very lives? Was it to prevent taxation without representation? After all, that's what most of us were taught in school, and it's true that "no taxation without representation" was a rallying cry of rebels. Was that *the* cause for which the Patriots were ready to fight and die? Did the Founders believe that death and disgrace were preferable to higher taxes, despite the fact that Englishmen paid far higher taxes than any American, and revenues from the new taxes were intended to defray the costs of defending the colonists from the French and Indians? Fomenting a revolution to ensure that your fellow countrymen must pay for *your* defense seems a bit unreasonable—if not childish.

In the 21st century, no serious historian really believes "no taxation without representation" was the underlying cause of the Revolution. This isn't to say that the colonists liked taxes. They certainly did not. But what they were actually rebelling against was not so much higher taxes but Britain's relatively recent (and rather ham-fisted) attempt to impose control over the colonies—colonies that were established generations earlier as largely self-governing bastions of liberty; utopian refuges from the mother country. Until the British government reorganized the empire, robbing the colonies of the autonomy they'd enjoyed for nearly two centuries, there was little talk of independence from England because

there was no need to seek independence from a country that had hitherto exercised little control over her distant territories.

What happened during the middle decades of the 18th century was
less a revolt against taxation than a growing realization among the colonists that they had developed a separate identity and culture from Great
Britain's. They had begun to realize that, by migrating to the North
American "wilderness," their ancestors had bestowed on them certain
liberties and advantages that the average British citizen didn't enjoy,
and with God's help, the proud and fiercely independent descendants
of those immigrants were not about to let the English wrest from them
control of their lands and their liberty.

The idea of *America* had entered the DNA of the colonists.

What the Patriots actually came to realize, what they actually resolved to fight for, was maintaining the independence they'd won generations earlier. The Revolution merely confirmed what many Americans
already knew in their hearts.

SWIMMING AGAINST THE TIDE

Conviction will almost always involve swimming against the tide of
popularity. In choosing his convictions, Adams' prescience was not
guided by popular sentiment. Though he was in the vanguard of a political movement that eventually swept the nation, he didn't rely on other
people's opinions. Instead, Adams' convictions stemmed from a finely
calibrated moral compass— a deep and abiding knowledge of what was
right and wrong. The values that most resonated with Adams were those
of his parents, his faith, his wife, and the community in which they'd
been nurtured—a community, by the way, that had *not* been founded
by a Royal Governor but by religious *separatists*. Even as a young man,
Adams had a strong sense of American identity and the potential for his
country to play a significant and separate role in world affairs. In October 1755, he wrote to his cousin Nathan Webb:

> *Soon after the Reformation, a few people came over into the
> new world for conscience sake. Perhaps this (apparently) trivial*

incident may transfer the great seat of empire into America. It looks likely to me. For if we can remove the turbulent Gallics, our people according to exactest computations, will in another century, become more numerous than England itself. Should this be the case, since we have (I may say) all the naval stores of the nation in our hands, it will be easy to obtain the mastery of the seas, and then the united force of all Europe, will not be able to subdue us. The only way to keep us from setting up for ourselves is to disunite us. Divide et impera. Keep us in distinct colonies, and then, some great men in each colony, desiring the monarchy of the whole, they will destroy each other's influence and keep the country in equilibrio.[32]

As an attorney, Adams boldly swam against the tide of popular opinion by agreeing to represent the British soldiers accused of murdering helpless citizens at the Boston Massacre of March 5, 1770—a move unlikely to burnish his reputation as a loyal Patriot.

No one else would take the case, he was told. Hesitating no more than he had over Jonathan Sewall's offer of royal appointment [he'd declined], Adams accepted, firm in the belief, as he said, that no man in a free country should be denied the right to counsel and a fair trial, and convinced, on principle, that the case was of utmost importance. As a lawyer, his duty was clear. That he would be hazarding his hard-earned reputation and, in his words, "incurring a clamor and popular suspicions and prejudices" against him, was obvious, and if some of what he later said on the subject would sound a little self-righteous, he was also being entirely honest...

Criticism of almost any kind was nearly always painful for Adams, but public scorn was painful in the extreme.

"The only way to compose myself and collect my thoughts," he wrote in his diary, "is to set down at my table, place my diary before me, and take my pen into my hand. This apparatus takes off my attention from other objects. Pen, ink, and paper and a sitting posture are great helps to attention and thinking."[33]

Adams defended the accused with a fervor bolstered by his personal belief that the soldiers had indeed been victims of the mob that brought on the incident. When the verdicts were in, Captain Preston and all but two of his men were acquitted. There were outcries against Adams in the newspaper and around dinner tables, but no riots. Though many disagreed with Adams' willingness to defend the soldiers, his reputation not only survived, it grew. Against the tide of public opinion and through the loss of half his clients because of the case, Adams followed his conviction that right is not guided by popularity. "Popularity was never my mistress," he would remark. Later, Adams would reflect back on this experience and call it "one of the best pieces of service I ever rendered my country."[34]

When conviction demands, leaders must be willing to go against the pressure of popular opinion. This is one of the hardest things a leader will ever do, because most inherently seek popularity. Real leadership, however, chooses to do what is right, no matter what others may think.

THE EARLY ADOPTER

John Adams was one of the first Patriots to consciously recognize that independence was the underlying cause for which they had taken up arms. It was this understanding of the greater vision behind "no taxation without representation" that prompted him to push for a separation from Great Britain. It was Adams' recognition of this worthy cause that led him to become an "early adopter" of the independence movement. In labeling Adams an early adopter, I'm not suggesting he was the sort who would camp out to get his hands on a new iPhone. Quite the contrary: Adams found himself again swimming against the tide on a "hot-button" issue.

Always the gadfly, Adams pushed the issue of independence relentlessly, and then he pushed some more and then some more. Once he became convinced of the need for independence, he held on to it as fiercely as a pit bull, ceaselessly prodding and lobbying members of Congress. There were times when the cause could have been defeated or shelved—when it seemed Adams was the only man in America interested in the issue. Still, nothing dissuaded him from seeking out any and every opportunity to buttonhole someone and talk up the merits of the cause. He did everything in his power to persuade the Continental Congress to come around to his way of thinking.

In February 1776, Adams had even jotted down a list of goals to be accomplished in Philadelphia later that year. From its placement in his diary, it appears it was composed earlier. It included "An alliance to be formed with France and Spain"; "Government to be assumed by every colony"; "Powder mills to be built in every colony and fresh efforts to make saltpeter." And, on the second of the two small facing pages in the diary, he wrote, a "Declaration of Independency."[35]

Convinced the cause was right, necessary, and in need of immediate action, Adams continued driving in the face of the "reasonable" objections from his fellow Congressman who asked, "Why all this hurry? Why all this pushing?" Even after Adams managed to cajole and persuade a majority of Congress to vote in favor of independence, even after "everything that could or need be said on the question of independence had been exhausted in Congress," he summoned the energy to continue the quest. Adams' deep conviction was clearly evident to all.

One final battle lay ahead. John Dickinson of Pennsylvania—one of the most eloquent opponents of independence—determined to make one last appeal for patience that July.

At 10 o'clock, with the doors closed, John Hancock sounded the gavel. Richard Henry Lee's prior motion calling for independence was again read aloud; the Congress resolved itself into a committee of the whole and "resumed consideration." Immediately Dickinson, gaunt and deathly pale, stood to be heard. With marked earnestness, he marshaled all past argument and reasoning against "premature" separation from Britain. "He had prepared himself apparently with great labor and ardent zeal," Adams would recall admiringly. "He conducted the debate not only with great ingenuity and eloquence, but with equal politeness and candor."

When he sat down, all was silent except for the rain that had begun spattering against the windows. No one spoke, no one rose to answer him, until Adams at last "determined to speak."

No transcription was made, no notes were kept. There would be only Adams' own recollections, plus those of several others who would remember more the force of Adams himself than any particular thing he said. That it was the most powerful and important speech heard in the Congress since it had first convened, and the greatest speech of Adams' life, there is no question.

To Jefferson, Adams was "not graceful nor elegant, nor remarkably fluent," but spoke "with a power of thought and expression that moved us from our seats." Recalling the moment long afterward, Adams would say he had been carried out of himself, "'carried out in spirit,' as enthusiastic preachers sometimes express themselves." To Richard Stockton, one of the new delegates from New Jersey, Adams was "the Atlas" of the hours, "the man to whom the country is most indebted for the great measure of independency...He it was who sustained the debate, and by the force of his reasoning demonstrated not only the justice, but the expediency of the measure."[36]

Thanks to the power of John Adams' unshakeable conviction and his perseverance against the headwinds of public sentiment, independence was achieved far earlier than it would have been otherwise... if at all.

The Roman Emperor Marcus Aurelius said, "Our life is what our thoughts make it." If so, then the nation in which we live today is largely the product of one man's thoughts: John Adams.

FAILING FORWARD

In developing perseverance and tenacity, there is no greater mentor than failure—or rather, the lessons learned from failure. Conviction does not imply that failures will not occur. Failure is a regrettable but inevitable part of life, no matter how deeply committed you may be to a particular goal.

Chuck Swindoll once said, "To lead greatly you must hurt deeply." Unless you've experienced difficulty, heartache, and opposition, you cannot know what you're made of, and may not survive the storms that will come your way.

Learning from failure and applying the lessons is mental and spiritual "weight training." As you lift the weights of failure, the resistance brings new strength to your mental muscles.

One of the best stories about exercising this kind of wisdom comes from Portia Nelson in her *Autobiography in Five Short Chapters:*

Chapter 1

I walk down the street. There is a deep hole in the sidewalk. I fall in. I am lost. I am helpless. It isn't my fault. It takes forever to find a way out.

Chapter 2

I walk down the street. There is a deep hole in the sidewalk. I pretend I don't see it. I fall in again. I can't believe I am in the same place, but it isn't my fault. It still takes a long time to get out.

Chapter 3

I walk down the same street. There is a deep hole in the sidewalk. I see it is there. I still fall in. It's a habit. My eyes are open. I know where I am. It is my fault. I get out immediately.

Chapter 4

I walk down the same street. There is a deep hole in the sidewalk. I walk around it.

Chapter 5

I walk down another street.

In *Failing Forward,* John Maxwell points out that the question is not *will you fail?*

If you don't fail, you're not really trying—you're not taking risks and exercising leadership. You're merely taking what comes your way. Leadership requires a résumé of failure. If you don't have a résumé of failure, you're either remarkably lucky, or possess Superman-like qualities, or you're not really trying. The question is not, "Am I going to fail?" The question is, "Will I get back up?" or, as Maxwell put it, "Are you going to fail forward?"

Reading newspapers and magazines today, I get the impression that younger people expect to become billionaires overnight—to succeed beyond their wildest expectations on the first try. Some people, as we have seen in the IT industry, seem to believe that success must be instantaneous and easy, or it will forever slip from their grasps.

That's our society in a nutshell—a microwave civilization in which impatience has become a virtue. In a world where email is no longer fast enough, people are becoming failure-averse, which translates into risk-averse, which translates into leadership-averse.

Aversion to failure...aversion to even the tiniest blows to our self-esteem makes us less resilient. When everybody wins a trophy, everyone becomes less capable of overcoming mistakes and failures. That should be a concern for all of us.

If you study history's greatest leaders or even watch the Biography channel on a regular basis, you'll immediately notice a pattern, a connection between most of these people. Few of them became overnight sensations. Many struggled for years, if not decades, to accomplish the feats and win the recognition that brought them fame. They failed, and failed often. They suffered. They sometimes came within seconds of giving up. But they didn't quit. They picked themselves off the mat and pursued the dream, or a different dream, or a modified version of the original dream.

Adams lost the first case he ever argued as an attorney. Had he been alive today, would he have put away his shingle and gone back to farming?

He might have, had his parents been the "helicopter" variety—the type that hover around their children to make sure they don't ever skin a knee or fail at a task. When it comes to their kids, the helicopter parent essentially says, "If boosting your self-esteem means doing your homework for you, I'll do your homework for you. I'll do everything I can to ensure your future success. If you forget to bring your lunchbox, it doesn't matter how many days you forget to bring it, I'll bring your lunch to school because I don't want my precious baby to starve."

Inadvertently, these parents are authoring a Greek tragedy. By vainly attempting to insulate their children from suffering and failure, they practically guarantee that the children will be unequipped to learn from their inevitable failures as adults.

You'll find helicopter parents in the business world, too. Some managers are always solving short-term problems for their employees and, by doing so, creating longer-term issues. There is certainly a place for helping employees and showing kindness to those who are struggling, but managers, like parents, must determine the best form of help. Sometimes doing nothing at all for your employee (other than allowing them to fail) is the best service you can render them in the long term.

Each day is filled with difficulties and even failures. It's okay. That's simply a part of life. When we become so afraid of failure, however, that we pass out trophies to avoid hurting anyone's feelings, we are engaging in self-defeating and unhealthy behavior. We are setting ourselves up for future failures from which it will be harder for us to learn and grow.

The science is clear. Awards can be powerful motivators, but nonstop recognition does not inspire children to succeed. Instead, it can cause them to underachieve.

Carol Dweck, a psychology professor at Stanford University, found that kids respond positively to praise; they enjoy hearing that they're talented, smart, and so on. But after such praise of their innate abilities, they collapse at the first experience of difficulty. Demoralized by their failure, they say they'd rather cheat than risk failing again.

In recent eye-tracking experiments by the researchers Bradley Morris and Shannon Zentall, kids were asked to draw pictures.

Those who heard praise suggesting they had an innate talent were then twice as fixated on mistakes they'd made in their pictures.

By age four or five, children aren't fooled by all the trophies. They are surprisingly accurate in identifying who excels and who struggles. Those who are outperformed know it and give up, while those who do well feel cheated when they aren't recognized for their accomplishments. They, too, may give up.

When children make mistakes, our job should not be to spin those losses into decorated victories. Instead, our job is to help kids overcome setbacks, to help them see that progress over time is more important than a particular win or loss, and to help them graciously congratulate the child who succeeded when they failed. To do that, we need to re-think all the meaningless plastic and tin destined for landfills. We have to stop letting the Trophy-Industrial Complex run our children's lives.[37]

WHEN THE HORSE IS DEAD, DISMOUNT

So where should the leader draw a line between perseverance and quix-otic delusion? Some pathways to the goal will be dead ends. How do you know you've reached a dead end? How do you know when it's time to stop wasting time with one approach and try something different?

There's an old saying: "When the horse is dead, dismount." That simple axiom is key.

Whatever the vision or goal, many of us can't recognize a dead horse, or we refuse to admit that the horse is dead. Instead of dismount-ing, we form a study group to analyze the dead horse, or we perform a reorganization of the dead horse. We fire old managers and employees and install new ones. We buy a better whip and beat the heck out of that dead horse, or we travel across the country, meeting with other compa-nies with dead horses to learn what they're doing with their dead horses.

As leaders, we must figure out when it's time to bury the horse and move on. This is when real wisdom is required. Not knowledge, not brainpower, but wisdom—insight into when the horse is really dead and when it merely needs to be nursed back to health.

There are three parts of a leader's body: the head, the heart, and the gut. Often, a leader will know in his head what should be done, but struggle with the heart to reach a decision. Sometimes the heart pulls him in one direction (e.g., hire a friend), but the head pushes him in another. A leader's most trustworthy friend is usually his gut. A leader's gut will often balance the head and heart when it's time to determine the right course of action. People always say "Trust your instinct," or "Go with your gut." However it's phrased, the message is clear: Listen to your gut, and you'll usually make the right decision.

A leader must discern between "this needs more effort," and "this will never go anywhere." For most of us, this requires keen intuition. You will *know* in your gut, and often in your mind and heart, when something isn't going to work.

Think about it. When you examine the facts and project forward, when you're really honest with yourself, you almost always know when an employee won't work out or a project won't succeed. You know it in your gut. On the other hand, your heart may work overtime to contradict the decision your gut is telling you to make. You don't want the employee to lose her job; you don't want to quit the project into which you've put so much effort.

It takes courage to quit after pumping a million dollars into a prototype or reorganizing the company around a new model, but there are times when you must. You *must* be able to say, "My heart says persevere, but my gut is telling me to try something else." You have to know when to detach from a particular path or version of your vision. You have to learn when it's time to take a different course.

Unfortunately, knowing when to keep fighting and when to switch course is easier said than done. Even John Adams occasionally failed in this respect.

In 1796, during Adams' first term as president, hostilities erupted between France and the United States. Known as the "Quasi War," the series of naval engagements between the newly formed French republic and the United States became *the* hot-button issue of the 1800 election. Adams refused to formally declare war, believing that peace *could* be achieved (and that war with France would be unwinnable). In the midst of the conflict, however, Adams' wisdom was overruled by his passion in the form of the Alien and Sedition Acts, the most damaging and damning legislative decisions of his presidency—a horrible stain on his otherwise virtuous record.

Enacted as war measures and based on widespread fears of enemy infiltrators, the Alien Acts were designed to prevent foreigners from becoming a "fifth column"[38] during the war. Any foreigner deemed dangerous could be expelled by the president, and the time required to naturalize new citizens was increased from five to fourteen years. In addition, aliens from countries with which the United States was at war could be deported without just cause.

The Sedition Act was meant to stop any "false, scandalous, and malicious" writings against the administration and the government. Like Lincoln some 60 years later, Adams believed that freedom of the press was absolutely necessary unless the nation was threatened by war. Silencing the opposition violated much of what Adams had passionately defended some 20 years before, but he stood by the legislation. Several editors were fined or imprisoned for their criticism of Adams' administration, while others were forced to close shop.

Adams violated his own sacred beliefs for the sake of expediency, but found himself and the nation no more secure than before. In the end, his failure to exercise wisdom cost him more than the election of 1800; it stained his reputation. Leaders must be able to discern when a conviction should be pursued with passion and when the horse, simply put, is dead. Know when to dismount.

In many ways, our current culture lacks conviction. Fear of offending or of being called narrow-minded often hinders people from letting their convictions guide them. Instead of passionately standing for what's right, many people choose to remain quiet, allowing "nature to take its course." Certainly there are times when wisdom must be exercised, but convictions are what drive people to go beyond themselves in the service of a greater cause. As 2 Thessalonians 3:13 (NIV) says, "Never tire of doing what is right."

Just as Adams was a man driven by conviction, we too must decide when and how to pursue the bigger vision. Adams knew that the risk of death was not only real, but likely. Yet his convictions concerning liberty moved him from the arena of fear to the battlefield of right. Our convictions, based on knowledge and wisdom, should be our motivators and our guides.

Thomas Carlyle said, "Conviction is worthless unless it is converted into conduct." This was the brilliance of Adams. He was able to turn what he believed into action. If we are to improve the world, our convictions must be translated into actions. Simple belief is only part of the equation. We must be willing to engage.

Great leaders have the faith to believe and the courage to do. You must ask yourself "What do I believe, and what am I willing to do about it?" If you're not willing to act, then you cannot call your belief a conviction. Conviction requires action. Otherwise it is simply another belief. Moreover, conviction cannot be denied or quieted. It cannot be ignored or muffled. True leaders not only develop convictions; they allow them to guide their words and deeds.

Are you a person of conviction or simply of belief? Do you allow your convictions to speak to your actions? Are you willing to stand alone for those convictions? Will you put them into action, no matter the cost? The answers to those questions may determine the measure of influence you have on your colleagues, your subordinates, your family, and your friends.

CHAPTER FIVE

ALEXANDER HAMILTON: EXECUTING THE VISION

T HE FORMER VICE PRESIDENT of the United States shoots and kills the former secretary of the treasury. While this may sound like the premise of a Tom Clancy novel, it actually occurred on July 11, 1804, ending the life of one of the most ambitious and unusual of the Founding Fathers.

Both of the non-presidents who appear on modern U.S. currency were self-made men. One was famous for his quips about thrift; the other for his financial leadership at the birth of the nation. One was born in the colonies and was slow to convert to the idea of independence; the other was born in the West Indies and was an early convert to the Patriot cause. Benjamin Franklin may be the better known of the two, but Alexander Hamilton played a larger role in shaping the federal government and steering the nation's financial and economic institutions onto a progressive and sustainable course.

Born in the British West Indies in 1755 or 1757,[39] Hamilton was the illegitimate son of Rachel Faucett Lavien and James A. Hamilton. His ignoble beginnings would haunt him all his days, and be used as a weapon against him in many political scrapes. Hamilton was abandoned by his father at a young age, and his mother died in 1768, leaving him, in essence, an orphan. Through a series of events and odd jobs, Hamilton ended up in the colonies, where he eventually enrolled in King's College in Manhattan (present-day Columbia University).

During the Revolution, Hamilton was Washington's aide-de-camp, which placed him at the epicenter of high-level military decisions, diplomacy, and negotiations. Eventually, he was given command of the New York light infantry battalion—a position that put him on the front lines at Yorktown, the battle that prompted the surrender of the British (and essentially ended the war).

Hamilton earned a living with his law practice and went on to serve the nation in Congress. Perhaps his greatest contribution to the nation, however, was his authorship of *The Federalist Papers*, still referenced today to shed light on the Founders' intentions. Later, Washington named Hamilton as the first secretary of the treasury, a position he used to lay the foundations of our modern economy.

Though famous for his financial prowess, Hamilton's greatest strength was his ability to translate his vision, and those of the other Founding Fathers, into reality. Above all, Hamilton was a practical idealist—a master of executing grand visions. He was not, unfortunately, a master of his own temper or his personal life. By July 1804 he had already participated in several duels, and Hamilton agreed to meet Aaron Burr on the same site in Weehawken, New Jersey, where his own son had been killed in a duel three years earlier. When the antagonists met, Hamilton fired over Burr's head, but Burr's shot hit Hamilton in the lower abdomen.[40] Hamilton died the next afternoon.

ACTIVITY IS NOT GOAL-FOCUSED PRODUCTIVITY

Good leadership = results. Execution is measured in terms of sustained progress toward the goals and objectives that add up to the ultimate vision. Vision execution is not about job descriptions, mission statements, hours logged, productivity figures, and the number of tasks you complete. Execution is about the nature and the quality of the activities completed and the quality of the results. Right now, your organization is perfectly calibrated for the results you are getting.

You probably know people who are always on the go. They are always busy, always scrambling to complete assignments, always too busy to talk...yet they never seem to accomplish much.

At one time or another, we all encounter this problem, but some people seem to spend their lives running faster and faster on the little hamster wheel without making much progress. When I ask you, "How was your day?" and you reply, "I had 100 emails and got through every one of them; it was a productive day" you are equating *activity* with *productivity*.

Too many employees and leaders mistake activity for goal-focused productivity.

Typically, the basis for this confusion stems from a leadership that doesn't recognize key results when they see them, because they don't know what they're trying to accomplish. They haven't developed a clear vision or haven't clearly communicated that vision.

Think of execution in terms of the following—a model I use frequently when I'm speaking to organizations.

Imagine that I've written on a whiteboard the word "vision" in the form of a traffic sign. This drawing centers on a road that moves you toward a vision. I draw a road that runs right into that vision, representing activities that propel us toward the vision.

I then draw a road that heads in the opposite direction, representing the things that detract us from achieving the vision. Both roads involve activity and motion, but one carries us farther away from the vision and the other takes us directly to realization of the vision.

Next, I draw a side road—like the exit ramp from a highway, which curves past the vision sign before heading off in an entirely new direction. This little road represents activities that distract us from the vision. They don't drive us away from the vision, but neither do they drive us to the vision. They may carry us close, but we will never reach the vision if we remain on that side road.

The church I pastor is located on a piece of property where we have built a sports complex. The highway leading toward the complex splits just before reaching the property. Both highways are named State Highway 121. One is SH121 Bypass and the other is SH121 Business. If you take SH121 Business you'll go near our property, but there's no way to actually get from there to the property. Only by taking SH121 Bypass will you be able to reach the property.

Although some activities will take us very near the vision, they will never take us *to* the vision. Activities that detract and distract may look good, but they represent roads to nowhere.

The final component of my model is a ditch that lies between the direct route to the vision and the road that detracts from the vision. This ditch represents the place in which many leaders and employees find themselves. When a car drives into a ditch, what happens? The wheels spin and the engine races, but the car sits still. There is a lot of activity and noise, but no progress. The ditch is the activities that drain the life from our vision. These activities drain our mental and physical energy. They drain us of the hope—and the will—to actually accomplish the vision. Many people spend their time doing things that seem to be driving them toward the vision, or that simply feel good, but they're merely racing their engines and spinning their wheels, even though it's getting them nowhere while it drains them of resources, energy, and time.

Do not mistake activity for goal-focused productivity. Not all motion is forward motion. Do not adopt an attitude of "As long as I'm moving, as long as there's activity, it must be a good thing." You must analyze whether that motion is taking you nearer or farther from the goal, or whether you're simply gunning the engine and spinning your wheels.

Measuring forward motion requires that you understand what the results of the vision should look like. Ask yourself, "What are the desired results? Specifically, what am I trying to accomplish?" If you can't list the anticipated outcomes of the vision in just a handful of words or sentences, you probably haven't articulated a clear vision—in which case, any old activity (bus) is fine because it doesn't matter where you're going.

Remember, "If the horse is dead, dismount." Too many leaders whip the horse, buy a new whip, hire consultants with whips, or study other companies with dead horses to learn "best dead-horse practices." They confuse activity with productivity. The horse is still dead and, short of a miracle, it's going to stay dead.

A THINKER AND A DOER

Like Alexander Hamilton, the best leader is both a thinker and a doer—a strategist and a tactician. At a minimum, CEOs must develop and articulate their visions before hiring the best COOs they can find to play Alexander Hamilton to their George Washington.

In any organization, it's essential that the leader says, "Here's what we've got to do, and here's the plan we will follow to get there." However, it's just as essential that the tactician says, "And *here* is the practical pathway we'll follow to execute that strategy. Here's *how* we will physically accomplish the strategy—step by step and month by month."

I recently talked with a friend who consults for a national restaurant chain. He said the CEO of the company likens tactics to boulders in a river. Tactics are the boulders we step on in order to ford the river toward the vision. The tactician determines the order in which we should step on those boulders, charting the best path to the vision.

It takes an unusual individual to be a strategist *and* tactician, but to some degree, every leader must try to be both. A strategist must dream. If you become mired in the "tactical mud," then you should revisit or reinvent the strategy to extricate the organization from that mud.

Leaders who rise to the very top are usually those with the ability to dream the big dreams. From there, they sketch the rough tactical blueprints needed to realize their big dreams. They needn't be especially detail-oriented, provided they locate and recruit detail-oriented lieutenants. They needn't be the kind of person who dots every "i" and crosses every "t," but they *should* have some sense of how the vision can be achieved before handing the reins to the people charged with executing the plans.

I analogize this strategy-to-tactics process to the plot of the movie *Apollo 13*. If you recall the movie (or real life), the ship in which the astronauts were circling the moon was damaged during flight. The situation was very tense, because the astronauts' lives were in jeopardy. Therefore, the vision for NASA's leaders was pretty simple: save the lives of three men. In one scene, the head of NASA tells all the engineers, "Look guys, you've got to figure out how to make this happen with the supplies the astronauts have on that ship." So the tacticians dump all the equipment actually on board the spacecraft onto a table, and from there they figure out what has to be done. They figure out which boulders have to be stepped on (and when) to accomplish the mission. In the end, the tacticians found a practical pathway for executing the vision.

Alexander Hamilton didn't accomplish his vision by leaving the details to others. He didn't rocket from obscurity—from unknown, illegitimate child to perhaps the most influential man in the federal government—by choosing the winning Powerball number or being in the right place at the right time. No, Hamilton had the exceedingly rare ability to quickly and simultaneously see "the forest *and* the trees." He was able to adopt both the long view and the short view, developing ingenious strategies and tactics that carried him toward his goal on the fastest possible track.

No episode better illustrates Hamilton's talents as a "vision executor" than his efforts on behalf of the federal government to assume the outstanding debts of the states. Proposed in his first treasury report of 1789, the "assumption" plan called on the federal government to assume the war debts of the states, which in turn would give greater leverage and power to the federal government. This plan generated swift and ferocious opposition among the Democratic-Republicans led by Thomas Jefferson.

Though political parties did not officially exist in the new United States at the start of George Washington's presidency, two competing visions of what America could and should be already existed. These were the ideologies around which the first two political parties soon emerged. The Federalists, whose spiritual and ideological father was Alexander Hamilton, dreamed of a strong central government largely modeled after that of Great Britain, but with certain improvements and refinements, including stronger checks and balances.

The anti-Federalists led by Thomas Jefferson (later the "Democratic-Republicans") dreamed of a loose federation of sovereign states whose weak central government was responsible for little more than national defense and resolving occasional disputes between states. While Jefferson and his followers believed that the best central government is one that governs the least, Hamilton and his followers were convinced that a robust central government was needed to support economic growth and forge a strong national identity from the disparate collection of former colonies.

The Federalists supported passage of the 1787 Constitution, which was designed to replace the Articles of Confederation, arguing their case most persuasively in *The Federalist Papers*, a project that Hamilton conceived and supervised. The anti-Federalists championed states' rights, and preferred to merely "tweak" the unwieldy Articles of Confederation. They bitterly opposed the adoption of the new Constitution.

During the Revolutionary War, the states spent huge sums of money battling Britain's military might. These expenditures were funded by issuing bonds to both individuals and financial institutions, American and foreign—including the Dutch and the French. With few exceptions (Jefferson's Virginia was one of them), the states had done a horrible job of managing their finances and paying off the debts—to the point where the phrase "full faith and credit of the United States" was practically a joke.

Hamilton believed the federal government should take on the debts of the states, which would put the national government in a much stronger position. As Hamilton began pushing through Congress some of the ambitious proposals featured in his first treasury report, Jefferson and his followers grew increasingly alarmed.

Jefferson feared that the funding scheme would create a fiercely loyal following for Hamilton among those enriched by it. He later told Washington that Hamilton had promoted a "regular system" of "interested persons" who were at the beck and call of the Treasury Department. He was convinced that congressmen were investing in government securities and that "even in this, the birth of our government, some members were found sordid enough to bend their duty to their interests and to look after personal rather than public good." Jefferson also did not believe that Hamilton really intended to pay off the government debt. "He wishes it never to be paid, but always to be a thing wherewith to corrupt and manage the legislature." This idea of perpetual debt flew in the face of Hamilton's express words and turned his funding program into a blatant grab for power.[41]

While Jefferson was correct that Hamilton's plan was in part politically motivated, Hamilton's desire to transfer the loyalties of "interested persons" to the federal government was no more nefarious than Jefferson's desire to *retain* their loyalties for state politicians.

Moreover, Hamilton had the vision and foresight to recognize that it was in the economic interests of the United States as a whole to prohibit the states from enacting a hodgepodge of duties and tariffs on imports and exports—not just between the states and foreign countries but between the states themselves. To become the economic juggernaut that the country eventually did, Hamilton foresaw that this taxing power must be reserved to the federal government. To become the empire of trade and industry that it eventually did, Hamilton foresaw that the federal government must have the ability to protect fledgling industries and fund public infrastructure projects, such as roads and canals, to support American commerce, rather than leaving it up to state and local governments.

Unlike Jefferson, who (like many in his party) was loyal first and foremost to his home state, which party members frequently referred to as their "countries," Hamilton was an adopted American who had no particular loyalty to any one state. His deepest loyalty was to the nation as a whole, which at that time was less a reality than a concept.

Whereas Jefferson and Madison feared the corrupting influence of centralized power, as well as any system based too closely on the British model, Hamilton abhorred the local "machine politics" he had battled in New York's capital of Albany, politics which in his opinion threatened to swamp the nation's identity and future growth in a tide of parochial self-interest. Despite Hamilton's Herculean efforts in the New York legislature during 1788 (including some of the most eloquent arguments he ever mounted in defense of anything), the Albany machine of Governor Clinton was so powerful (and so opposed to ceding power to an enhanced federal government) that the state adopted the Constitution only after its passage was assured.

In short, Hamilton and Jefferson each believed that the other man's faction was motivated by selfish interests, riddled with corruption and hell-bent on strangling the infant republic in its cradle.

In this context, it's no wonder Jefferson later characterized the fight over the assumption as "the most bitter and angry contest ever known in Congress before or since the union of the states," and that on four separate occasions between February and July 1790, "Madison thwarted attempts to enact assumption." People whispered into Hamilton's ear that Madison was jealous of his power, that Madison coveted his job... Hamilton's funding plan brought state loyalties to the surface. Some states, such as Massachusetts and South Carolina, struggled with heavy debts and were glad to be relieved by the central governments. Others, such as Virginia and North Carolina, had settled most of their debts and saw no reason to help. Such differences threatened to explode the brittle consensus that had been so arduous to reach at the Constitutional Convention.[42]

By the end of April 1790, it appeared that the Jefferson-Madison faction had beaten Hamilton. The House of Representatives had voted down the assumption plan and also decided to discontinue all debate on the issue.

Hamilton was dejected. But he wasn't beaten.

He never took his eyes off the prize—off this seemingly minor component of his larger vision—because he knew that the assumption plan was a key "boulder" on the path to the grander vision. In the short term, the assumption plan would help him establish a strong credit rating for the nation. In the long term, the plan was a critical stepping stone toward the formation of a robust national government that could shepherd the struggling American economy from insignificance to one that must be reckoned with on the world stage.

It was at this point, therefore, that Hamilton launched a search for leverage—for a prize he could hand the anti-Federalists in exchange for passing his assumption plan. He soon found his bargaining chip in the issue of where to permanently locate the national capital, an issue as contentious as that of the assumption.

The location of the U.S. capital was already a subject of intensive lobbying and animosity, because the winning state would be blessed with an immediate influx of money, population, and economic activity. Despite his nationalist leanings, Hamilton was initially determined that the capital remain in New York City, where he lived—a determination that intensified after he became part of Washington's cabinet. Meanwhile, the anti-Federalists associated New York with Alexander Hamilton and his faction so much that they sometimes referred to the state as "Hamiltonopolis."

In the spring of 1790, the controversies over the location of the capital and the assumption plan became so vicious that the union threatened to break apart.

It was now that Hamilton had to choose which vision was more important. He didn't hesitate. Without question, it was the assumption. In early June, after the House enacted his funding legislation *without* the assumption component, he looked for ways to strike a compromise. According to Jefferson, after bumping into Hamilton outside Washington's residence, the men decided to dine together that night.

If we are to credit Jefferson's story, the dinner held at his lodgings on Maiden Lane (Manhattan) on June 20, 1790, fixed the future site of the capital. It is perhaps the most celebrated meal in American history, with guests including Jefferson, Madison, Hamilton, and perhaps one or two others. Despite his dislike of assumption, Jefferson knew the stalemate over the funding scheme could shatter the union, and as secretary of state, he also feared the repercussions for American credit abroad.

Madison restated his familiar argument that assumption would punish Virginia and other states that had duly settled their debts. But he agreed to support assumption—or at least not oppose it—if something was granted in exchange. Jefferson recalled, "It was observed...that as the pill would be a bitter one to the southern states, something should be done to soothe them." The sedative measure was that Philadelphia would be the temporary capital for 10 years, followed by a permanent move to a Potomac site. In a lucrative concession for his home state, Madison also extracted favorable treatment for Virginia in a final debt settlement with the central government. In return, Hamilton agreed to exert his utmost efforts to get the Pennsylvania congressional delegation to accept Philadelphia as a provisional capital and a Potomac site as its permanent successor.[43]

Both sides kept their ends of the bargain. Our capital is indeed located on the Potomac and the federal government assumed the states' debts, becoming the sole entity in charge of regulating interstate and international trade.

Some historians debate which side got the better deal, but I believe Hamilton was the clear victor. Although some people say a bargain would have been struck relatively soon thereafter, with or without the background negotiations, and that Hamilton "caved" before it was necessary, I think America could use more "caving" of that sort. Hamilton, as well as Jefferson and Madison, showed a great deal of political and personal maturity in agreeing to compromise. Hamilton, especially, displayed a character trait that contemporary business and government leaders should emulate—the ability to recognize which "boulders" represent the critical steps along the visionary pathway, as well as those that can be sidestepped.

Ideological and philosophical purity may win plaudits from pundits and hyper-partisan supporters, but the type of all-or-nothing conquests required to realize "purist" visions are exceedingly rare and often undesirable.

Hamilton was nothing if not pragmatic. Ivory tower thinkers have the luxury of holding fast to their theoretical dogma, but men like Hamilton—men determined to translate ideals into realities—know that executing a vision requires realistic, cold-eyed, horse-trading pragmatism. Leaders must have the conviction to know when to refuse compromise, but they must also possess consensus-building skills when compromise truly *is* the best option.

THE POWER OF SELF-DISCIPLINE

Hamilton exercised so much discipline in pursuit of his goals that it's almost unfair to suggest him as a role model to anyone who hasn't been blessed with the intellect of an Einstein and the talent of a Mozart.

For example, the task of writing *The Federalist Papers* was originally split among Hamilton, James Madison, John Jay, and several other prominent men who supported the new Constitution. Each man was to draft essays corresponding to his area of expertise—e.g., the history of republics, foreign policy, finance—which would then be reviewed and edited by the other members before submission to the newspapers. The 85 essays totaled 175,000 words, and were originally published in installments over the course of seven months. In the end, however, Hamilton shouldered most of the burden. He wrote 51 of the essays to Madison's 29 and Jay's five.

Extolled as a literary and political masterpiece, the creation of *The Federalist Papers* is all the more amazing when you consider that Hamilton already had his hands full with his law practice, and that he and Madison were under serious deadline pressures. As Ron Chernow notes in his biography of Hamilton, "The first of the staggered series of [state] ratifying conventions was scheduled to start in late November [1787], and this allowed Hamilton and Madison little opportunity for fresh research or reflection. They agreed to deliver four essays per week (that is, two apiece) at roughly three-day intervals, leaving little time for revision. The essays then appeared in four of the five New York newspapers. The constantly looming deadlines meant that the authors had to draw on information, ideas, and citations already stored in their minds or notes...So excruciating was the schedule, Madison said, that often 'whilst the printer was putting into type parts of a number, the following parts were under the pen and to be furnished in time for the press.' Very often, Hamilton and Madison read each other's contributions in print."

At one point, Hamilton muscled out 21 essays in a two-month period. On two occasions, he published five essays in a single week, and on one occasion he published six in a week. Hamilton's original papers reveal that many of the essays sprang from his brain in near-final form, with few strike-outs or revisions.[44]

Despite their enduring influence, *The Federalist Papers* were not written for posterity. They were essentially written as op-ed pieces—as topical works of journalism with the sole object of winning political support (at the state level) for the new Constitution.

The amazing self-discipline Hamilton exercised to complete this project is something every leader should strive to emulate rather than just envy. After all, you can't run a marathon without training, and you can't get to Carnegie Hall without practice.

I'm not suggesting that you drive yourself to an early death, but I do suggest that you drive yourself. Consider the level of determination and goal-focused activity that will be needed to realize your vision, and be prepared to make sacrifices of time, money, and effort as you "train" to run the marathon that is your vision quest. This is where wisdom is critical. A leader must strike a balance between two sayings. One is, "Don't set sail when the wind isn't blowing." The second is an old proverb: "When the wind isn't blowing, row."

EVERY LEADER NEEDS A GOOD MENTOR

Even a man as multi-talented and disciplined as Alexander Hamilton did not rise from his lowly origins without considerable assistance, without the invaluable coaching and mentoring that began when Hugh Knox, pastor of a Presbyterian Church in St. Croix, steered him toward a life of scholarship. One piece of Hamilton's early writing, a letter about a hurricane that devastated the island, so impressed local business and community leaders that they took up a subscription fund to send him to America for an education. Within a few years of Hamilton's arrival in New York, George Washington (perhaps the most influential—if not the only—father figure that Hamilton ever knew) took him under his wing during the Revolutionary War as his aide-de-camp.

We often forget (or fail to realize) that everybody needs a coach; everybody needs a mentor. It doesn't matter who you are, we all need mentoring.

The need for coaching is most obvious and visible in sports. Great athletes are always associated with great coaches. Without Vince Lombardi, would Bart Starr have ever reached the level he achieved? Without Red Auerbach, where would the Boston Celtics have gone? Would UCLA have done what they did without the leadership of John Wooden? Even golfers such as Tiger Woods and Rory McIlroy need a coach.

To quote the Bible, "As iron sharpens iron so one man sharpens another." Proverbs 27:17 (NIV). Sometimes we don't know what we don't know, and we need somebody to tell us what we need to know. Tiger Woods sometimes needs to fix his swing, but without a coach, he might not identify the mechanical flaws that need to be addressed.

Not long ago, I took my son to a baseball coaching session; he participated in a specialized coaching program for kids his age. As I watched the coach instructing my son, I recalled meeting a batting coach for the Texas Rangers. He coaches players who've been to the World Series—men who still recognize that they need a coach to help them extract their maximum potential. It occurred to me that we all need someone to show us the things that we cannot see for ourselves. Whether we are amateurs or professionals on top of our game, everyone needs a coach to help reach the next level.

We all need the self-discipline to execute, and that self-discipline is usually instilled in us by someone else. We aren't born self-disciplined. We need mentors to enter our world, so we can learn to become self-disciplined and learn to better execute.

We also need to tap into our mentors' networks of friends, colleagues, and acquaintances, so we can be connected to opportunities for exercising our talents and self-discipline. Hamilton would have gotten nowhere without his St. Croix connections and (later) the connections he made through Washington.

If you do not already have one, find a mentor in your life. Everyone needs three people in life—someone who is ahead of you on the road of life, who can mentor and encourage you on the journey, someone who is behind you on the road—someone whom you mentor and encourage—and someone to befriend you and walk with you as you journey through life.

Mentoring and competition can also sharpen your skills and talents (not to mention your mind), provided you respond to them properly. Hamilton faced so much opposition to his policies and programs in his later years that he had no choice but to sharpen his intellect, his arguments, and his tactics to have any hope of achieving his goals. He couldn't afford to be lazy and trust only to luck in his pursuit of those goals. Jefferson and the anti-Federalists weren't about to roll over in awe of his considerable intellect.

Hamilton had to stay one step ahead of the opposition. He had to be resilient.

INTUITION AND EXECUTION

This brings us back to the subject of "smart failure."

Failure is inevitable...assuming you actually try to accomplish anything. If you don't try anything, you're obviously not going to fail. When you try things, however, you open up the possibility of learning something. You will either fall apart or develop greater strength.

Consider an egg, a potato, and a teabag. What do these three things have in common—other than being breakfast foods?

For one, all of them are frequently placed in hot water.

If you put an egg in hot water, it becomes firm on the inside. A lot of people, when they confront difficult situations, react like the egg—they become hardened on the inside. And everyone knows that these people are hardened on the inside, because they are often bitter and difficult to be around.

If you put a potato in hot water, it becomes softer, and eventually turns to mush and falls apart. A lot of people turn to mush when they encounter difficult or stressful situations. Most people know when someone is falling apart, but they are often unsure how to help.

However, if you put a bag of tea in hot water, it rises to the occasion and changes its environment.

The bag of tea shows the way to become more resilient. When you encounter difficulties and failures in life, chances are you'll respond like the egg, the potato, or the teabag. You're either going to fall apart or become hardened—or rise to the occasion and change the environment. Hamilton may have let himself harden on the inside like an egg; he never turned to mush like a potato, but he definitely changed his environment like a bag of tea.

The purpose of learning to be resilient is to accomplish something more than mere survival. Resilience is about learning to *thrive*, learning how to respond to similar challenges in the future, learning how to rise to the occasion in the midst of failure. People like to say that "success goes to your head and failure goes to your heart." Learning to be resilient ensures that the lessons learned by the heart will seep into the head.

How do you learn from your mistakes?

That requires you to do something that few people bother to do—taking time to objectively analyze your past actions.

Take the time to use your "Ben Franklin powers" of self-awareness to figure out the where, when, how, and why of your mistakes. What were the reasons for the failure? How could they have been prevented? Who dropped the ball and why?

More often than not, the reasons for failure rest squarely on your shoulders. To paraphrase Shakespeare, the fault lies not in your stars but in yourself. Maybe you were too greedy; maybe you overlooked a "minor" detail (a hidden boulder on the pathway to success), or maybe you aren't very good at executing visions and need to recruit someone like Hamilton for the team—the kind of person who knows how to get stuff done. One of my best career decisions was hiring people who are much smarter than I am. This ensured that we would accomplish our shared visions.

I counsel couples who are experiencing marriage problems. Unlike some counselors, who start the first session by asking one spouse, "So what's your problem with your spouse?" I always ask each one in turn, "What's *your* problem? What are *you* doing that's causing the problems in the relationship?" That question always takes people aback because they usually come to the session thinking, "I'm not here to talk about me. I'm here to beat up the other person."

You can learn from your mistakes if you can be objective—if you take the time to really reflect on the causes of the mistakes and really look for solutions. More importantly, you can learn from your mistakes if you have the *desire* to learn something. This process isn't about finding someone to blame (including yourself), but about recognizing patterns and habits and tendencies that produced the past failures, as well as ideas for defeating those patterns, habits, and tendencies so they aren't repeated in the future. It's also about recognizing something we all know, but few of us take to heart—that no one is perfect, tomorrow really *is* another day, and the seeds of opportunity lie in the ashes of yesterday's defeats.

Head decisions, heart decisions, and gut decisions are different. Do not underestimate your "gut feelings" when analyzing and overcoming self-defeating patterns, habits, and tendencies. Intuition is one of mankind's most valuable and frequently underrated abilities. Though it's often presented as a spooky art, intuition is anything but spooky. The ability to predict outcomes with a fair (or even an astounding) degree of accuracy has nothing to do with ESP, witchcraft, or "spirit vibes" emanating from the astral plane or some other dimension.

Intuition is nothing more than a form of unconscious reasoning, according to biological anthropologist Helen Fisher—one "rooted in the way our brains collect and store information. As you accumulate knowledge—whether it's about what books your spouse likes or how to play chess—you begin to recognize patterns."

The brain unconsciously recognizes and organizes patterns into blocks of information. Over time, the brain identifies and links to more and more of these patterns, storing the clusters of knowledge in long-term memory. When you see a tiny detail linked to a familiar pattern, you immediately recognize the larger pattern. *That* recognition is what we call a "flash of intuition," or "gut feeling." It is the ability to size up people and situations.

Fisher recommends that people listen to their gut feelings instead of brushing them aside. "Your intuition may not always steer you right, but it can be a useful first step in decision-making," she says. "Intuition is really learned expertise in disguise. So if you've played tennis your whole life, go with your instinct on the court instead of thinking through each stroke."[45]

Unlike "magic powers," intuition requires an extensive knowledge of the people, environments, and situations you're dealing with. Because identifying patterns requires prior experience with the patterns, *including patterns of failure*, it is useless in encounters with new individuals, unknown environments, and unfamiliar situations. For example, if you've managed a department or a company long enough, and gotten to know your peers and subordinates, it's likely you've developed an uncanny talent for predicting how different people will react in different situations.

When you delegate a project that needs to be "done yesterday" (try to avoid this whenever possible, by the way), you will *know* that Kelly will remain calm and take a methodical approach to the work, but Larry will probably freak out. However, if you hire a brand-new employee, it's initially impossible to predict how the person will react, because you don't have any prior knowledge of that employee's personality and character traits.

In the business world, in the sports world, and in family life, experience equals power—*provided* you have thoroughly and correctly analyzed the lessons of experience. Knowledge can lead to understanding, and understanding can lead to wisdom, and wisdom is the basis for smart decision-making.

DO YOU NEED MINIONS?

Is it better for visionary leaders to delegate grunt work to trusted "minions" rather than waste time and effort on tasks for which they have no talent? As a Jefferson or a Washington, is it more cost-effective to search for your very own Alexander Hamilton rather than trying to develop or hone these skills yourself? Should bosses devote less time to self-improvement and more time to "finding your Grant," as Donald T. Philips suggested in his book *Lincoln on Leadership*?

Yes and no.

Some tasks *must* be the sole purview of the leader, though many others can be delegated. For example, it would have been an abdication of his responsibilities as commander-in-chief for Washington to have assigned a subordinate the task of deciding whether to abandon New York to the British in late 1776. That was an executive-level decision, a decision for the supreme military chief. However, it was perfectly appropriate for Washington to delegate the logistics of the retreat to his subordinates.

Every leader needs his tacticians. Every leader needs different people—different mixtures of skills and talents—to accomplish different missions.

My church, an organization with total annual revenues of more than $6 million, needs an accountant. I can't understand math that requires anything more complicated than basic multiplication. Accounting is just not my strength. So I have people who handle every bit of that work for me. I oversee the process, and I'm aware of the big picture, but I don't handle the details. And that's as it should be.

All leaders need people who can compensate for their own personal and professional shortcomings. The best leaders hire people smarter than they are. Don't let your ego get in the way; if you have smart people around you, it won't make you look bad—it will make you look smarter than you really are.

I sincerely doubt that any of the Founding Fathers would have named George Washington as the "brainiac" of the group. Washington was by no means a dummy, but he would never have been voted "smartest person in the Founders' club." He wasn't a leader by virtue of raw intelligence. For sheer intelligence, one would have to choose among Jefferson, Hamilton, Franklin, and probably John Adams.

But clearly Washington was the *leader*. And clearly he was intelligent enough and self-confident enough, and he had enough self-awareness to install people around him who could get the job done better than he could himself. He knew himself well enough to recruit officers and (later) cabinet members who shored up his own intellectual and skillset deficiencies.

Great leaders must be able to do that. At the same time, while opposites attract, opposites also attack. This is a lesson Washington learned as a general and as president. Some of the traits you found endearing about your spouse or a subordinate early in your relationship can later become the most annoying traits you've ever known. That's just human nature.

A leader must be smart. He has to use his head and know when to ask, "Do I need a Hamilton in my life? Who do I know who can take on this function or task?"

To some extent, leaders must be both strategists and tacticians, planners and executors. An organization can rise only as high as the leader. If the leader limits the organization through the quality of the people he puts around him, the organization will not arrive at the destination defined by the grand vision.

Alexander Hamilton's whole life is an example of translating strategies and tactics into practical paths to success. He could have spent his life as a forgotten clerk in what eventually became a Caribbean backwater. Instead, he developed a vision of something much larger than the life he had known, and devoted himself to finding pathways to achieve that vision. Chernow comments:

> In all probability, Alexander Hamilton is the foremost political figure in American history who never attained the presidency, yet he probably had a much deeper and more lasting impact than many who did...
>
> As the first treasury secretary and principal architect of the new government, Hamilton took constitutional principles and infused them with expansive life, turning abstractions into institutional realities. He had a pragmatic mind that minted comprehensive programs.
>
> In contriving the smoothly running machinery of a modern nation-state—including a budget system, a funded debt, a tax system, a central bank, a customs service, and

a coast guard—and justifying them in some of America's most influential state papers, he set a high-water mark for administrative competence that has never been equaled.

If Jefferson provided the essential poetry of American political discourse, Hamilton established the prose of American statecraft. No other founder articulated such a clear and prescient vision of America's future political, military, and economic strength or crafted such ingenious mechanisms to bind the nation together.[46]

CHAPTER SIX

THOMAS PAINE, SAMUEL ADAMS, AND PAUL REVERE: GETTING YOUR MESSAGE OUT

IN REAL ESTATE, THE CONVENTIONAL WISDOM is that success depends on "location, location, location." In business leadership, however, that wisdom translates to "communication, communication, communication." Absent mental telepathy, clear and persuasive communication is the only tool for motivating, inspiring, and directing people.

Let's focus on three Founders whose achievements personify the best practices of leadership communication.

THOMAS PAINE: APPEALING TO HEARTS AND MINDS

Most Americans know very little about Thomas Paine, despite the profound impact his ideas had—and still have—on our government and national identity. The work Paine published during the Revolution was pivotal in inspiring colonists separated by geography, history, and religion to unite behind the common causes of independence and democracy. Probably no other writer of pamphlets or books had as much influence on U.S. public opinion, until Harriet Beecher Stowe wrote *Uncle Tom's Cabin*.

Born in England in 1737, Paine was apprenticed to his father, a corset maker. He wasn't much of a go-getter, though, and his early career is marked by one job problem after another. In 1774, Paine moved to Philadelphia and became a magazine editor. A champion of oppressed peoples, he frequently wrote anonymous letters condemning the slave trade.

After the battles at Lexington and Concord, Paine began work on a pamphlet that was published in January 1776. In *Common Sense*, Paine eloquently argued in favor of American independence. The pamphlet was an instant sensation, selling more than 500,000 copies in a few months at a time when the population of the country was only three million. One historian called *Common Sense* "the most incendiary and popular pamphlet of the entire revolutionary era."

Following the success of *Common Sense*, Paine produced a series of short papers that became known as *The American Crisis*. These papers opened with the famous words, "These are the times that try men's souls." The work was so powerful that Washington ordered it be read aloud to the troops at Valley Forge.

Ultimately, Paine traveled back to Europe where he wrote *The Rights of Man* and *The Age of Reason*, two famous tracts that influenced the French Revolution and the cause of reform in Europe. He later returned to America, but discovered that his fame had waned. Although Paine's notoriety had faded, the impact and power of *Common Sense* lived on.

The ideas articulated in *Common Sense* were neither unique nor especially original. Many of his arguments were the same as those the Patriot "intelligentsia" had been debating for some time. What distinguished *Common Sense* from every previous published article, pamphlet, and letter was its electrifying appeal to the common man. In *Common Sense*, Paine captured the *heart and mind of the average person,* not just the political elite of the era, inciting them to adopt the cause as their own and take action.

Yes, Paine's arguments were brilliant and eloquent, but more importantly, they were emotionally compelling. They incited deeds as well as words.

In *Common Sense*, Paine's objective was not merely to engage in an academic exercise. He had more in mind than positing a well-crafted thesis and supporting it with well-reasoned arguments built on logic and references to great classical philosophers. He had more in mind than a pamphlet that would spur dialectics among "eggheads" over Madeira and quail at the local taverns. No, Paine's goal was to educate, persuade, and inspire *the masses* to join the independence movement. He wanted laborers and farmers, merchants and sailors, coopers and rope makers, seamstresses and schoolteachers to open their hearts and eyes and see the vision that he could so clearly see. He wanted them to believe what he believed, and understand why the cause mattered to each and every one of them.

To accomplish these goals, Paine did something few of his contemporaries had managed to do...or had even attempted:

1. He focused on just two points—independence from England and the creation of a democratic republic.

2. He avoided flowery prose and instead wrote in the language of the people, often quoting scripture in his arguments. Most people in America had a working knowledge of the Bible, so his arguments rang true. Paine was not religious, but he knew his readers were. King George was "the Pharaoh of England" and "the Royal Brute of Great Britain." He touched a nerve in the American countryside.[47]

Paine accomplished something in *Common Sense* and *The American Crisis* that every leader should strive to emulate. He gave voice and purpose to the widespread, but as yet undefined and unarticulated, hopes and yearnings of his countrymen. He shone a spotlight on a vision that many Americans already shared—in their hearts—but didn't have the skill to express in simple but eloquent form. Essentially, Paine said what was already on the minds of many people. He said to the masses, "Isn't this the vision you've always had for yourself and your families, even if you couldn't articulate it? Aren't these the ideals to which we've already devoted our lives? If so—if this is the vision and these are the goals we all have for America—let's move forward to make this vision a reality!"

When it comes to getting the message out; when it comes to articulating and disseminating your vision, I can't overstress the importance of using simple but compelling language—words and ideas that appeal to hearts and minds, as well as heads and hands; language that inspires and motivates people to dedicate themselves to a cause. In my experience as a pastor, teacher, and public speaker, the single worst mistake made by most leaders is assuming that appeals to logic alone are sufficient motivation. I'm not suggesting you toss logic out the window, or behave like a demagogue by tapping into people's base instincts and biases, but I *am* stressing the need to appeal to deeper feelings and desires. To illustrate my point, consider these opening sentences from *The American Crisis*:

> *These are the times that try men's souls: The summer soldier and the sunshine patriot will, in this crisis, shrink from the service of their country; but he that stands it now, deserves the love and thanks of man and woman. Tyranny, like Hell, is not easily conquered; yet we have this consolation with us, that the harder the conflict, the more glorious the triumph. What we obtain too cheap, we esteem too lightly: it is dearness only that gives every thing its value. Heaven knows how to put a proper price upon its goods; and it would be strange indeed if so celestial an article as freedom should not be highly rated.*

Now compare Paine's writing with these sentences from a blog written by a management consultant trying to persuade freelance service providers to make statistical analysis part of their planning process:

> *The global employment report for Q1 of 2013...has some impressive macro statistics. The report starts with two upwards trending growth curves that illustrate jobs posted and Freelancer earnings. Both show a nice, almost linear growth, but with a slight upturn in both jobs being posted and earnings more recently. The quarterly comparison between Q1-2012 and Q1-2013 is particularly interesting. The baron Q1-2012 looks more than half the size of the bar for Q1-2013 but the*

dollar amounts for year-to-year below do not seem to reflect this. The quarter-to-quarter for registration seems to suggests a fairly consistent trending from about twice the freelancers registering than clients (consistent with the gross numbers reported) back in Q1-2012 to over two and one half times the number of freelancers than clients registering in Q1-2013... Freelancer enrollments are indeed outpacing client enrollments and this trend seems consistent. This may suggest for you that steeper competition is looming...

Obviously, I'm comparing apples and oranges here. It's not entirely fair to compare Paine's impassioned plea to discouraged American Patriots with a blog designed to persuade entrepreneurs to pay more attention to online hiring statistics.

If your communications resemble the latter instead of the former, I recommend you keep the following tips in mind:

- KISS (not the old band but the old axiom: "Keep It Simple Stupid")

- Know your audience.

- Determine why the audience should care. Obviously, some messages are important whether anyone cares or not, but for people to be inspired, they need to care. Your words should communicate why people should care.

- Whenever possible, choose simple, active, and direct sentences instead of passive, compound, and complex sentences.

- If you can't summarize the central premise of the communication in one or two sentences, head back to the "mental drawing board" until you can.

- Favor short Anglo-Saxon words over polysyllabic Latin-derived words.

- If you must use jargon and "20-dollar words" to demonstrate you're the smartest person in the room, you probably aren't.

Can today's leaders hope to duplicate the kind of inspiration, passion, and dedication to a cause that Thomas Paine elicited?

The answer is yes—you can, and you should.

Leaders must find their inspirational voices. They must harness their followers' energies by articulating a collective vision on their behalf. How clearly you communicate the message will directly affect how well you inspire your followers, which will directly affect the results.

TURN CRISES INTO OPPORTUNITIES

Leaders must locate their own voice and communicate their vision in that voice, especially during a crisis. It was during crises that Thomas Paine truly excelled at inspiring people. His methods offer a lesson in turning negatives into positives, which is critical when you need to rally the team behind your proposed solutions.

Unless you keep people perpetually in the dark, almost everyone will be aware of the problem or crisis soon after it occurs. What they may *not* know is what to do about it. Your people may not see the full extent of the problem or crisis, and they may not have the same perspective from the trenches that you have from your position, but they know things aren't good. FDR didn't have to tell Americans they *had* a problem after the Japanese sent half the Pacific Fleet to the bottom of Pearl Harbor. What he needed to do was tell them *what they could do about it.* He needed to transform the disaster into an opportunity that inspired the nation to rise to the occasion.

If a new product bombs or it appears the company is going under, the leader must help employees see the opportunities produced by the seeming disaster. And a leader can do that by taking control of the terms of the debate—something we hear about during presidential debates ad nauseum.

Paine defined the debate by clearly defining the problem as he saw it, not as the opposition saw it. *This is our problem with the Crown. This is how we have been mistreated. This is what's wrong.*

> *I challenge the warmest advocate for reconciliation to show a single advantage that this continent can reap by being connected with Great Britain. I repeat the challenge; not a single advantage is derived. Our corn will fetch its price in any market in Europe, and our imported goods must be paid for by them where we will. But the injuries and disadvantages which we sustain by that connection, are without number; and our duty to mankind at large, as well as to ourselves, instruct us to renounce the alliance: because, any submission to, or dependence on, Great Britain, tends directly to involve this Continent in European wars and quarrels, and set us at variance with nations who would otherwise seek our friendship, and against whom we have neither anger nor complaint. As Europe is our market for trade, we ought to form no partial connection with any part of it.*

What Paine did was speak to the masses right where they were. As a communicator, you must also provide clarity on the endgame—on what you're trying to accomplish. You must focus on desired outcomes. Simple, forceful arguments will give you the advantage. They will also allow you to take control of the conversation.

> *The authority of Great Britain over this continent, is a form of government, which sooner or later must have an end: The most powerful of all arguments, is, that nothing but independence, i.e., a continental form of government, can keep the peace of the continent and preserve it inviolate from civil wars.*

Here Paine took control of the discussion. After stating the problem, he then offered the solution. The ability to control the dialogue and shape the message is what separates good leaders from mediocre leaders. Abraham Lincoln did this during the Civil War; initially he had but one focus in conducting the war: to restore the Union. That was it. That was his singular focus. According to Lincoln, if he could destroy slavery and save the Union, he would do so. If he could keep slavery and save the Union, he would do so.

Later, as the war progressed, he added another focus to the grand vision: abolishing slavery. As the war dragged on, he realized the need to end the evil of slavery. But in his messages, he never failed to focus on either the one goal or the other. In this way, he maintained control over the national dialogue. He didn't allow the Confederates to turn positives into negatives or to distract the northern public from his interpretation of the issues. He didn't allow Jefferson Davis to successfully characterize the war as a squabble over states' rights and tariffs.

Lincoln made sure that when the northern public thought about the war, they thought in terms of restoring the Union and (later) restoring the Union and ending slavery.

Men such as Thomas Paine, Sam Adams, and Paul Revere weren't interested in winning debating points by refuting British viewpoints one rebuttal at a time. Determined to persuade as many colonists as possible to their point of view, they turned each crisis of the 1760s and 1770s into an opportunity to advance their agenda and to cast the opposition's agenda in a tyrannous light.

PERSUADERS ARE SALESMEN

With persuasive communications, most people are tripped up by two common problems: (1) they get bogged down in details and minutia or in the symptoms of problems instead of the causes and solutions; and (2) they don't know how to *sell their ideas*.

Persuasion is the art of selling ideas and inciting actions. Like every good salesman, Paine focused on selling his audience *first* on the benefits of his "products" and *second* on the features. Most people do precisely the opposite.

Pay a visit to your local electronics shop, and you'll witness this sort of backward salesmanship—the reverse of Paine's approach to persuasion. Approach the nearest salesperson and tell him that you need a computer system for your home or small business and see what happens. Chances are, he'll rattle off facts and figures about the number of giga-bytes, gigahertz, megapixels, and USB ports that each computer features without explaining what any of this means to you—without explaining how you'll benefit and *why you should care.*

A friend recently told me the story of buying a GPS unit for his car. When he asked the salesman for advice, the salesman began talking about the features. After several minutes, my friend interrupted. "Look, I just want the GPS to get me from here to there without having to look at a screen. Will a woman's voice talk to me? Will she give me enough notice before I have to make an emergency right turn onto a highway ramp?"

Many salespeople elaborate on the 50 features the consumer will never remember to use rather than the one or two things that will make the product indispensable in the customer's mind.

Paine talked about the big issue facing America, British tyranny, and how Americans would benefit by separating from the mother coun-try. He focused on the benefits Americans could expect as an indepen-dent and democratic people—and only afterward did he discuss some of the features of that republican form of government. *That* is first-class salesmanship.

Paine also knew something that today's leaders should internalize: Communication must be constant and regular. Most people's enthusi-asm will inevitably flag. Therefore it's up to the leader to rekindle the flame of passion over and over again through frequent and timely com-munication.

SAM ADAMS APPEALED TO HANDS AND FEET

While Thomas Paine was focusing on Americans' hearts and minds, Sam Adams was aiming straight for their "hands and feet." He was slightly less focused on *why* Americans should fight for their liberty and more focused on *what* they should be doing to obtain it.

When most people think of Samuel Adams, it's not for a revolu-tionary cause but as a product spokesman for a brand of beer. But Samuel Adams was far more than a mascot on a label of suds—he was less about beer and more about fire.

Often confused with his more famous cousin John, Samuel Adams was born in Boston, the son of a brewer. Though he grew up in the home of a merchant, Adams struggled with business. His real success came in public office. He served as a tax collector for the Crown, which allowed him to establish a wide variety of acquaintances throughout the Boston community—a network of influential connections. While serving in the Massachusetts Assembly, he proposed the outlandish idea of forming a "continental congress," a national legislative body to which he was later elected.

Adams was known for his outstanding oratory and was considered a fire-breather as he rallied an audience. While the Revolution was still in its infancy, the British government targeted Adams as a troublemaker and sent troops to Lexington to find him and his financier John Hancock. Many credit Adams' passionate oratory for prompting the Sons of Liberty to stage the famous Boston Tea Party.

Adams was a man who understood that great accomplishments do not simply happen: They require people inspired to action. More than most people during the early days of the Revolution, Samuel Adams carried the torch for independence and lit flames in the hearts of his countrymen. As he once said, "It does not require a majority to prevail, but rather an irate, tireless minority keen to set brush fires in people's minds."

How did Adams appeal to people's hands and feet? Why was he the consummate rabble-rouser of the Revolution?

I think that was just the way he was wired. Some people are introverted and some are extroverted. Sam Adams buried the needle on the extroversion scale. He had an innate ability to rally people to his causes, motivating them to get the job done. But without the hearts and minds part of it, without the reason and passion that Paine brought to the table, persuading people to tackle a job won't accomplish much. Adams' specialty was the stuff of riots and revolts rather than successful revolutions.

In Chapter 1, I mentioned a gentleman named Simon Sinek, who invented a model known as the "Golden Circles." Sinek notes that most leaders work from the outside of these concentric circles. They start by asking "What *is* it that we do?" before moving inward to ask "How are we going to do it?" and many of them never consider *why* they do anything.

Thomas Paine, I believe, worked from the inside out. He wondered, "Why are we doing this?" before he considered, "How are we doing it?"

I believe Samuel Adams worked from the outside in. He said, "This is what we're going to do. We're going to organize a group of people to throw rocks at British troops" or, "We're going march to a 'Liberty Tree' and burn an effigy of the governor while singing patriotic songs and guzzling barrels of beer and wine."

There are plenty of people who sit around and never get anything done. They sit in their ivory towers and ponder the issues. Then there are people who just do stuff. They check off boxes on their action lists, but those boxes may or may not be connected to the vision the organization is trying to accomplish. These Action Johnnies don't really care, because that's not what they do. They do their jobs, they check off their lists, they move on.

Both thought and action are necessary to achieve a vision. Therefore, every organization needs *both* types of communication—the Thomas Paine and the Samuel Adams variety.

USE A MIX OF MEDIA FOR YOUR MESSAGES

One of my friends is a public relations veteran who's written many new business proposals. He believes Samuel Adams was the most astute "spin master" of the Founding generation. What most distinguished Adams' public relations efforts was his exploitation of every communications medium at his disposal, something modern PR firms do as a matter of course but many other organizations never even consider. "When I write new business proposals," says my friend, "I start by reviewing with a boilerplate list of the different public relations techniques available to me. Looking at Samuel Adams' career, my first thought was, 'Man, this

guy really knew how to play the game! He employed every communications medium and tactic he could find on the 18th-century menu—
something from columns A, B, and C.'"

The lesson from Sam Adams is: Don't restrict your communications
to just one or two media. Adams used every technique in the modern
PR playbook to get his messages out, including:

- Press releases (pamphlets).

- Op-ed pieces (sometimes disguised as "news").

- Anniversaries and celebrations.

- Demonstrations, parades, and protests.

- Speeches, songs, and symbols (parade floats, liberty trees, flags,
  silverware).

- Alcohol and tobacco (not recommending this, just pointing
  out a fact).

Use every communications tool appropriate to the message. If the
only tool in your box is a hammer, you'll probably view every problem
as a nail.

Figure out how to continually communicate the message to keep
people motivated and inspired—to keep those hands and feet in action.
Package and repackage that message in different ways. Many leaders get
attached to the hammer in the toolbox. *I'll just use a hammer to fix everything. It doesn't matter what it is.* They must realize that people now learn
and respond to messages very differently than previous generations did.

Adams didn't limit himself to pamphlets and letters. He used
the print media, he used speeches, he used songs and symbols (flags,
liberty trees, engravings, and silver cups) as well as lots and lots of
alcohol. If Adams were alive today, he'd be using Facebook and Twitter
and LinkedIn...as well as demonstrations on Wall Street or outside the
United Nations headquarters.

ADAMS CONSTANTLY SOUGHT SPRINGBOARDS

Adams never missed an opportunity to capitalize on a crisis or a British mistake. He exploited every misstep or gaffe he could find (or manufacture) for use as a message springboard, beginning with the Stamp Act of 1765. The 13,000-word piece of legislation required that a duty be paid on almost every piece of paper used in the colonies, including legal documents, newspapers, almanacs, bills of lading, and playing cards. Many colonists were (to put it delicately) dismayed by the new revenue-collection scheme, and some—including Adams and a group that became known as "The Loyal Nine"—responded with acts of civil disobedience and even violence. While some disaffected colonists protested the Stamp Act in writing, Adams and the Loyal Nine chose action. They hanged an effigy of the local stamp master, Andrew Oliver, from an old tree, and the tree soon became known as the "Liberty Tree."

"In the coming months and years, Liberty Trees sprouted or were so labeled in Braintree, Petersham, Great Barrington, and Cambridge, Massachusetts; Newport and Providence, Rhode Island; Norwich, Connecticut; Annapolis, Maryland; and Charleston, South Carolina. But it all began a short walk from Samuel Adams' home in the South End of Boston, at what was described as a 'stately elm...whose lofty branches seem'd to touch the skies.'"[48]

But this act of protest by Adams and his compatriots didn't end there. The effigy was allowed to hang from the tree for a full day with an attached sign that read "He that takes this down is an enemy to his country." After thousands of people had an opportunity to view the symbolic act of defiance, the Loyal Nine instigated something more tangible—they encouraged a crowd of Stamp Act opponents to vandalize the homes of Oliver and the Lieutenant Governor of the colony, Thomas Hutchinson.

"On the evening of August 26, 1765, a mob burst in on Hutchinson's brick mansion in Boston, and 'smashed in the doors with axes, swarmed through the rooms, ripped off wainscoting and hangings, splintered the furniture, beat down the inner walls, tore up the garden, and carried off into the night, besides £900 sterling in cash, all the plate, decorations, and clothes that had survived, and destroyed or scattered in the mud, all of Hutchinson's books and papers.'"[49] Though Adams' role in the riots is still debated, many historians believe that (at a minimum) he incited the mob to riot even if he didn't directly participate in trashing the houses of Oliver and Hutchinson.

Whatever the case, Adams didn't stop there. Using a variety of methods and media including published letters, private correspondence, meetings, speeches, and grassroots organizing, Adams and his comrades fomented protests and such widespread flouting of the law that the Act was repealed in less than a year. During this period, he even broached in writing the idea of American independence—more than 10 years before his cousin John successfully pushed the cause through the Continental Congress.

With the repeal of the Stamp Act, most Americans today would probably high-five their buddies and go back to business as usual. Not Adams.

He understood that this was only the beginning of the struggle. Because he also understood that most of his fellow citizens would let the matter drop once the dust settled, he did everything in his power to keep the rabble continuously roused. Among other things, Adams turned the anniversary of the first protest against the Stamp Act into an annual celebration marked by parades, songs, feasting, drinking, networking, and speechifying. There were always new effigies to hang, and floats were even constructed for parades. Below is an account of the August 1769 celebration of the Stamp Act resistance told from the perspective of Paul Revere. (By this time, the Loyal Nine had become the Sons of Liberty.)

> ...[Revere] and the other Sons of Liberty converged around the Liberty Tree at eleven in the morning. Up went the glasses and out went the toasts, one after another, until fourteen were said. They upped the king and queen, America and the Sons of Liberty...and they imprecated 'the Traducers of America' and 'the late abandoned Fugitive,' by whom they meant the governor. Once the toasts were completed, they crossed Boston Neck in a string

of more than a hundred carriages and settled into an afternoon in Dorchester and Lemuel Robinson's Liberty Tree Tavern. On the field by the tavern, the Sons set up two rows of tables and stretched a sailcloth overhead. Colorful banners fluttered in the breeze and musicians sawed off tunes.

Paul moved among the crowd, seeing one friend and then another. Several were customers, many fellow Masons. There was Joseph Warren. Cousin Thomas Hitchborn...

And Samuel Adams and John Adams...And still more patriot leaders, like Thomas Young and William Palfrey, John Hancock's clerk. There was John Hancock himself, decked out like a prince. Even John Singleton Copley—no radical he—mixed among the throng. In all, the crowd numbered more than 350. ...Three whole pigs were barbecued for the occasion, plus chickens and codfish. And cups of Madeira too. After dinner came the toasts—forty-five in all..."Success to the Manufacturers of America!" "The Speedy Removal of all Task-Masters, and the Redress of all Grievances!" "The Liberty of the Press!"[50]

If Adams and Revere seem like men adept at organizing and leading a fraternal organization, it's because many of those men *were* members of established fraternal organizations such as the Masons. These memberships taught them how to quickly and effectively communicate, as well as organize boycotts, demonstrations, and the occasional riot.

Samuel Adams especially reminds me of the old-time bosses of Tammany Hall and politicians such as Lyndon Johnson. Like them, Adams was skilled in spreading his messages at the grassroots level and organizing people for immediate action. He knew who the "movers and shakers" were among the Patriots, as well as the opposition, and he knew how to influence people through a variety of means. In a word, he knew how to network. This is how Adams transformed ideas into actions.

In the years ahead, Adams and the Sons of Liberty marked other notable events leading up to the Revolution with more feasts, parades, songs, monuments, souvenirs, and engravings—many of them crafted by Paul Revere. The most famous engraving commissioned by Samuel Adams, and produced by Revere, was that of the so-called Boston Massacre, an incident that features Adams the "spin master" at his most brilliant.

In my office, I have a trivet on which Revere's famous engraving of the massacre is reproduced. In his depiction of the incident, the only aggressors are the British soldiers, muskets blazing into the hapless crowd. The only people killed or wounded are the stunned civilians—a fine, upstanding, and innocent-looking bunch.

In fact, the Boston Massacre of March 1770 was the culmination of a series of running street battles between (frequently outnumbered) Loyalists and British soldiers and gangs of thugs and ne'er-do-wells. On March 5, a lone private named Hugh White was guarding the Custom House when a boy insulted White's captain. White cuffed the boy in the head with his musket. Shortly thereafter, with the moon rising over the snow-covered streets of Boston, church bells began ringing and cries of "Fire!" filled the area. As crowds poured into the street, Private White called for reinforcements. Eight more soldiers soon came to White's aid, led by Captain Thomas Preston.

The red-coated British troops set up in a semicircle facing the crowd. The people were calling them "Lobsters" and taunting the soldiers, goading them to fire, a cry that mixed with the fire alarms still in the air. Then a chunk of ice—a snowball, a club or a stick, or perhaps an icicle or hard slab of snow from the roof of the Custom House—hit Private Hugh Montgomery. He fell to the ground, and whether by accident or in frustration, he discharged his musket into the crowd. The other soldiers fired, too, in a chain reaction. Captain Preston initially did not order them to stop. In a few minutes, five colonists were fatally wounded, and as the Bostonians scattered and rushed to tend to their casualties, the British troops marched back to their quarters.[51]

Adams sprang into action, spinning the incident as an unprovoked massacre of innocents. Adams and his fellow Sons of Liberty unleashed an avalanche of private and public letters; Adams commissioned the famous engraving from Revere within hours and pressured local judges to arrest and try the soldiers posthaste. Adams then covered the trial as a journalist, publishing tens of thousands of words on the proceedings—all crafted to win sympathy, if not outraged support, for the Patriot cause.

Although many Americans know that Revere engraved the image of the infamous "massacre," what's less known is that the original illustration was the work of one Henry Pelham, another local engraver and painter. "It's a large and emotionally striking picture that shows redcoats arrayed against the people, their guns leveled in a professional manner, the words 'Custom House' behind them, over their shoulders, establishing the scene. Great blasts of smoke cloud the scene, the weapons discharged on the order of a commander raising his sword. The people are fallen back, some down on the ground with wounds issuing blood; some helping others; some simply dead. It wasn't how the men actually fell, nor how the soldiers stood; Revere's diagram of the scene makes that clear. But it communicated what the people of Boston felt—that the event was a deliberate act of murder." [52]

For reasons still unknown, Pelham dropped off the illustration with Revere, who proceeded to copy the work *and* embellish it in a way that would further inflame people's passions. For example, Revere eliminated the words "Custom House" inscribed over the building and substituted the words "Butcher's Hall." Pelham was upset by the changes (and perhaps more upset that Revere immediately began selling copies of the engraving), and he fired off a stinging letter of rebuke. To this date, Revere's version of the event, called "The Bloody Massacre," is the more famous of the two illustrations.

EMOTION IS A POWERFUL MOTIVATOR

If Thomas Paine's messages targeted hearts and minds, Adams' messages targeted the spleen. By making people angry and infusing them with righteous indignation, he sought to incite acts of protest and even violence. He didn't simply communicate *why* colonists should revolt against their British overlords, but *what* they should do about it, as well as when and how. He didn't just argue in favor of revolt, he urged people to physically do it—tomorrow, in the town square, and don't forget the torches and tar and feathers.

Emotion is a powerful motivator. At the same time, emotions are rarely easy to manage—like those of the Boston mob. In addition, Sam Adams-style "spinning" can wreak havoc with the truth, and ultimately with one's credibility. The key to effective messaging is telling the facts in ways that promote your vision without spinning them so far that they become outright lies or distortions. There is nothing wrong with telling the truth about your vision. Your job as a leader is to not only paint the picture of your vision, but to do so with compelling words and calls to specific actions.

For Adams, however, the truth was whatever he wanted it to be. In this respect, I doubt he would succeed today, not in this era of Internet-enabled fact-checking. Today, lies and half-truths backfire more often than they succeed. As an article in *The Atlantic Monthly* recently noted, "that point is crucial."

> *If the director of the CIA can be caught in a lie, anyone can. More than ever before, our communications leave trails. Whether we imagine them to be "digital exhaust," as many tech theorists do, or fodder for a bits-based Big Brother, as Orwell might have, our Facebook timelines and e-mail chains and cellphone logs are leaving copious and minutely detailed records of our lives. Which means that the claims we make about ourselves, from the big to the banal, can, as never before, be cross-referenced against reality. Stuck in traffic? This real-time map suggests otherwise. Never got the email? The sender's read receipt begs to differ. You're 25? That was true, a Google search says—five years ago. Whether we're communicating via clay tablets or telegraph wires or fiber-optic cables, our deceptions are kept in check by an overarching fact that has little to do with technology and everything to do with community: we want other people to trust us.*[53]

One of Adams' key strengths was that he never missed an opportunity to send a powerful message, because he was laser-focused on achieving his vision whenever and however possible. Unfortunately, his penchant for distorting the truth (also one of his strengths) is today a glaring weakness. Adams' brand of spin-doctoring was possible only in an era when great distances and low-tech communications media didn't permit for fast and equally powerful rebuttals. In the 18th century, the Patriot story was whatever Samuel Adams needed the story to be. That approach doesn't wash anymore. Contemporary leaders must walk a tightrope between intelligently promoting their interpretations of reality and distorting the truth so badly that followers will react with cynicism or even disengagement from the cause.

Today's leaders must be straight shooters, because modern Americans are more skeptical about advertising and public relations claims, no matter how these messages are transmitted and by whom. More and more people have become convinced that everyone is trying to sell them a bill of goods. They're being lied to so often and so cleverly that a widespread resentment has developed—and it's getting harder and harder to overcome.

Adams had the ability to frame issues in ways that often deviated from the facts—far from the facts. Today he would probably be challenged often and effectively by average citizens as well as his political opponents. Many of his arguments would be neutralized, and it's possible that he would even be marginalized as a crackpot.

Adams was a great patriot and ultimately his cause was liberty and freedom, but to a certain extent his behavior was unsavory...to put it mildly. He was the least "classy" of the Founding Fathers, if you care about that sort of thing. He's not the man you put on currency, but the one you put on beer bottles. As critical as his involvement in the Patriot cause was to the Revolution, Adams may have gone too far in his pursuit of the vision.

But I'm grateful that Adams was on our side. If I needed someone to stir up a crowd and incite people to action, I wouldn't hesitate to hire Sam Adams if he were alive today, but I *would* hesitate to invite him to my home for Thanksgiving. He'd probably insist on watching cable TV news instead of football, and then complain about how so-and-so was out to destroy the country, "so let's hit the streets and burn their house down."

PAUL REVERE'S INFORMATION SUPERHIGHWAY

What most people think they know about Paul Revere is that he rode a horse and screamed at the top of his lungs that the British were coming.

> *Listen, my children, and you shall hear*
> *Of the midnight ride of Paul Revere,*
> *On the eighteenth of April, in Seventy-Five;*
> *Hardly a man is now alive*
> *Who remembers that famous day and year*
> —Henry Wadsworth Longfellow,
> "Paul Revere's Ride"

Revere most certainly did *not* scream "the British are coming" (he and the listeners were all part of the British Empire), but his shouts did awaken the people of Massachusetts, as well as the people of the other 12 colonies, to the coming revolution.

Revere was well-known in Boston because he was a successful businessman, silversmith, and passionate defender of the colonists' rights. He was so passionate, in fact, that he took part in the Boston Tea Party and was a member of Boston's Committee of Safety. Revere was influential in business, and worried that British "oppression" of the colonies was negatively impacting everyone's bottom line. He knew that a change had to be made.

However, it was his famous midnight ride that ensconced Revere forever in American lore. What most people don't know, though, is that Revere was not the only rider that night. In fact, he was unable to complete his journey because he was arrested (briefly) by the British. Revere accomplished his primary mission, but without the help of two companions, William Dawes and Samuel Prescott, many Minutemen would have learned too late about the approaching redcoats.

Revere wasn't one of the original "Loyal Nine" who organized the first protests against the Stamp Act, but he was well-connected with its members, who traveled in the same circles he did. He joined the Sons of Liberty in 1765, and thereafter supported the Patriot cause by producing engravings and other propagandistic items. In addition to his engraving of the Boston Massacre, his work includes a depiction of British troops arriving in Boston in 1768 (which he called "an insolent parade"), as well as "The Liberty Bowl." The bowl was crafted in honor of the 92 members of the Massachusetts House of Representatives who refused to rescind a letter protesting the Townshend Acts of 1767, which taxed tea, paper, glass, and other products. The act of civil disobedience by the "Glorious Ninety-Two" was a major step toward the Revolution. The bowl was commissioned by 15 members of the Sons of Liberty, whose names are engraved on the bowl. The Liberty Bowl, the Declaration of Independence, and the Constitution have been called the nation's three most cherished historical treasures.[54]

During the mid-1770s, Revere and a group of "mechanics" (skilled laborers) began meeting in secret at a favorite tavern, the Green Dragon, to coordinate intelligence gathering and dissemination. Among other things, they frequently tracked the movements of British troops. Revere's midnight ride was merely the most famous of these intel-dissemination missions.

On the night of April 18, 1775, in response to reports that British troops were preparing to march to Lexington to capture John Hancock and Samuel Adams, as well as secreted caches of weapons, ammunition, and powder, Revere and Dawes made their way to Lexington to alert the leaders to the imminent danger. En route, Revere warned other patriots, many of whom then set out to deliver warnings of their own.

Here's a little-known fact: by the end of that night, as many as 40 riders were spreading the news of the British army's advance.

But Revere never shouted "The British are coming!" because his mission required the utmost secrecy and the countryside was filled with British patrols. According to eyewitness accounts and Revere's own recollections, the actual warning was "The Regulars are coming out."[55]

Revere arrived in Lexington around midnight, and Dawes arrived about a half hour later. They met with Adams and Hancock, who escaped just ahead of the British soldiers. Revere and Dawes rode on to Concord accompanied by Samuel Prescott, a doctor who happened to be in Lexington "returning from a lady friend's house at the awkward hour of 1 a.m."[56]

But Revere, Dawes, and Prescott were quickly detained by a British patrol at a roadblock; Prescott and Dawes managed to escape (though Dawes soon fell from his horse and was unable to complete the ride). Questioned by the British at gunpoint, Revere did a rather remarkable thing: He told the truth. He said British troops would be in danger if they approached Lexington because the militia were gathering there.

Later, as he and other captives were being led toward Lexington, a gunshot was heard. When the British officer demanded that Revere explain, he replied that it was a signal to alert the Patriots. Apparently, Revere believed he had nothing to gain from lying—either that or he feared that lies would be quickly revealed and severely punished.

What stands out regarding Revere's ride (other than its reflection of the Patriot system of disseminating "actionable news" known as "alarm and muster," which was developed months earlier in response to a notable failure), was how he enlisted other men to help him spread the message. The lesson of Revere's ride today is less about Revere and more about Dawes, Prescott, and the 40 other men who spread out like "web spiders" across a rural network of roads, Indian trails, and farm fields—the information superhighway of 18th-century Massachusetts. Without those other riders, the intelligence would not have reached as far and as wide as it eventually did. As it was written in Ecclesiastes 4:9-12 (NIV):

> *Two are better than one, because they have*
>   *a good return for their labor:*
> *If either of them falls down, one can help the other up.*
> *But pity anyone who falls and has no one to help them up.*
> *Also, if two lie down together, they will keep warm.*
> *But how can one keep warm alone? Though one may be*
>   *overpowered, two can defend themselves.*
> *A cord of three strands is not quickly broken.*

Another lesson from the episode is that *everyone* can make a difference.

Revere wasn't a leader of the Patriot cause. He was a talented goldsmith/silversmith, but he was no Sam Adams, John Hancock, or George Washington. Nevertheless, he displayed uncommon conviction, devotion, and commitment to the movement and to his comrades, volunteering to do his part without complaint. While he wasn't always happy playing the role of supporting actor, especially after the war began, his grumblings never interfered with his efforts—in stark contrast to the would-be Founding Father who is the subject of the next chapter.

Revere's life reveals that you can be a normal guy, an average Joe, and still play a pivotal part in the success of the vision and the prosperity of the organization. Your participation can be even more critical to the success of your organization, at times, than that of the CEO. Washington, Adams, Jefferson...none of those men did what Revere and his fellow "everymen" accomplished that night in April. This achievement was Revere's alone. He "took ownership," as businessmen like to say today.

Employ each and every member of the organization to help you spread your message. Don't be shy about requesting assistance from the future Paul Reveres under your command. The brilliance of Paul Revere's approach was that he had a message that needed to get out, but he didn't insist on hogging the glory. Too many leaders want the "news and information" to come only from their mouths, or be distributed only after it's approved their offices. Great leaders understand that when your vision goes viral, you will accomplish far more. Multiplication always trumps addition when it comes to getting your message out.

As individuals, Thomas Paine, Samuel Adams, and Paul Revere played smaller roles in the Revolution than giants such as Washington, Jefferson, and John Adams, but collectively they served as one of the most potent public relations, marketing communications, and recruitment groups in history. Without their efforts to inspire the heads, hearts, and hands of so many colonists, the Founding Fathers' grand vision would have remained just that—a vision.

CHAPTER SEVEN

BENEDICT ARNOLD: THE DARK SIDE OF LEADERSHIP

IN THE CHAPEL OF THE U.S. MILITARY ACADEMY at West Point, just above the choir loft, 12 black marble plaques gleam in the dim light. On each of the stone shields, which memorialize generals of the American Revolution, four lines are engraved: name, date of birth, rank, and date of death. One of the plaques, however, has just two lines: "1741" and "Major General."[57] This is the shield that was meant to honor Benedict Arnold, but it never has. And it never will. Arnold sacrificed his honor and the cause of independence on the altar of his ego.

I think it's fitting that the plaque sits alongside those of Arnold's former comrades in arms. It serves as a tragic reminder about the life of Benedict Arnold—a man who could have been one of the most revered figures in American history but lost his honor after deciding to serve a cause only as large as himself.

Born in Norwich, Connecticut, Arnold was raised in the home of a successful businessman who turned to alcohol after the deaths of three of his children. This, along with great financial strain, induced young Benedict to leave home and apprentice as an apothecary. Within a few years, he became a local merchant and then an international trader. By the age of 22, he had earned enough money to buy back the family homestead, which had been sold to pay his father's debts. He then resold the property for enough profit to buy a fleet of ships.

In the decade before Lexington and Concord, Arnold had opposed the "oppressive" British taxes and policies that disturbed so many others, and he came to lead the local chapter of the Sons of Liberty. When the Revolutionary War started in April 1775, Arnold joined the Continental Army and quickly teamed with Ethan Allen and his Green Mountain Boys to capture the British garrison at Fort Ticonderoga in upstate New York.

Later in 1775, Arnold led a military expedition on an epic march from Maine to Quebec in a disastrous effort to rally the Canadian people behind the Patriot cause and deprive the British of a northern base. The enlistments of many of his soldiers would expire on New Year's Day, however, so Arnold decided to launch a desperate attack against heavily fortified Quebec City during a blinding snowstorm on December 31, 1775. Shortly after the fighting commenced, however, he received a grave wound to his leg and had to be carried from the field. The assault failed, and Canada remained in British hands.

By late 1776, Arnold had recuperated sufficiently to return to the field. He played a critical role in forestalling a British invasion of New York by correctly predicting that British General Guy Carleton would sail his forces south along Lake Champlain. To counter this strategy, Arnold oversaw the quick assembly of an American fleet on the lake to meet the British invasion force. On October 11, 1776, Arnold and his men surprised the British and, though Carleton's flotilla drove off the Yankees, the farsighted attack delayed the British approach long enough to prevent them from making any further gains that year—18th century armies did not campaign during the winter. Thanks to the Battle of Lake Champlain, Patriots were saved from potential disaster.

Despite this valiant service, Arnold didn't receive the recognition he believed was due him, and when Congress promoted five junior officers over him, he resigned from the army. He agreed to return only at Washington's urging. Fortunately, Arnold rejoined the military just in time to participate in the defense of central New York from an invading British army led by General John "Gentleman Johnny" Burgoyne in October 1777.

In the battles against Burgoyne, Arnold served under General Horatio Gates, an officer whom Arnold came to hold in contempt. The antipathy was mutual, and Gates at one point relieved Arnold of his command. Nonetheless, at the pivotal Battle of Bemis Heights on

October 7, 1777, Arnold defied Gates' authority and took command of a group of American soldiers whom he led in an assault against the British line. Arnold's attack threw the enemy into disarray and contributed greatly to the American victory. Ten days later, Burgoyne surrendered his entire army at Saratoga. News of the surrender convinced France to enter the war on the side of the Americans. Once again, Arnold had brought his country a step closer to independence. However, Gates downplayed Arnold's contributions in his official reports and claimed most of the credit for himself.[58]

Arnold was again seriously wounded—in the same leg that had been injured at Quebec—a wound that rendered him temporarily incapable of commanding troops in the field. While he was recovering in 1778, Washington appointed him to the position of military governor of Philadelphia. It would prove a fateful decision.

Arnold enjoyed the city's bustling social life, hobnobbing with prominent persons—some of them with Loyalist sympathies. Worse, he seems to have violated various civilian and military regulations to enrich himself, arousing the suspicions (and later denunciations) of state officials. Rumors spread through Philadelphia that Arnold was abusing his position for personal profit. In addition, during this time, Arnold courted and married a young woman (his first wife had died) named Peggy Shippen, the daughter of a man suspected of Loyalist leanings.

Arnold and Peggy enjoyed a lavish lifestyle, and they accumulated significant debts. These debts, along with the simmering resentment Arnold felt over the slights to his reputation, were among the factors that seem to have motivated Arnold to betray the American cause. At some point, he decided that his personal interests would be better served by helping the British rather than suffering for an army and a Congress that he believed were ungrateful. That point was probably reached after charges of misconduct and corruption were filed against him with Congress. Although some of the charges were dismissed, Arnold was convicted on four relatively minor counts, which earned him a mild rebuke from Washington. In Arnold's mind, however, his reputation had once again been sullied, his achievements ignored.

By late 1779, Arnold had begun secret negotiations with the British to surrender the American fort at West Point, New York, in exchange for £20,000 and a command in the British army. Unluckily for Arnold, his chief intermediary, British Major John André, was captured in September 1780 while crossing between British and American lines disguised in civilian clothes. Papers found in André's boot incriminated Arnold in the treasonous plot. Learning of the capture, Arnold fled to the British lines before the Americans could arrest him. For his part, André was hanged as a spy in October 1780.

THE PATH BETWEEN SELFISHNESS AND SELFLESSNESS

Arnold was one of the most driven men of the Revolution. He was also one of the most easily hurt. His feelings were easily damaged and his ego easily bruised. And as the saying goes, "Hurt people *hurt* people."

Arnold was hurt and that hurt went to his heart, after which it migrated to his head and his "hands and feet." Eventually, Arnold chose self over everything else, and came up quite empty. Following his betrayal, he received some of the money promised by the British, along with a commission in the army. He later led raids on Virginia and New London, Connecticut, before sailing with his wife and baby to London. Back in England, however, he still didn't receive the recognition that he thought his due. As it turns out, nobody likes a traitor, even if the betrayal was in the service of *your* cause.

As a result, Benedict Arnold, once a contender for "great hero of the Revolution," will forever be known as the American Judas Iscariot.

Though leaders must be driven to pursue their visions at great cost, leaders driven by a shaky sense of self-worth are headed for a world of pain—a world of receiving *and* inflicting insults, slights, and affronts. What Arnold's life reveals about leadership is the potential within all of us to exhibit the dark side of leadership. We see the positive side of power reflected in the life of George Washington and the negative side in the career of Benedict Arnold. In the end, personal character determined which side would triumph in each man.

In *The Chronicles of Narnia*, C.S. Lewis wrote about the nature of power. Lewis tells the story of four children's journey to the mythical land of Narnia. When the three Pevensie children meet Mr. and Mrs. Beaver, they first hear of the great lion Aslan.

> *"Ooh!" said Susan. "I'd thought he was a man. Is he quite safe? I shall feel rather nervous about meeting a lion."*
>
> *"That you will, dearie, and make no mistake," said Mrs. Beaver, "if there's anyone who can appear before Aslan without their knees knocking, they're either braver than most or else just silly."*
>
> *"Then he isn't safe?" said Lucy.*
>
> *"Safe?" said Mr. Beaver. "Don't you hear what Mrs. Beaver tells you? Who said anything about being safe? 'Course he isn't safe. But he's good. He's the King, I tell you."*

Power is never safe. Like fire, when used for good, power can benefit many, but when used for evil, it can leave behind a trail of destruction. Wherever there is power, there is potential for abuse.

What are the warning signs that leaders should watch for—the early red flags that we may be pursuing a vision or activity for the wrong reasons? In my experience, the biggest warning sign that you're veering toward the dark side is that your vision, goals, strategies, or tactics are designed to satisfy the ego. When the issues are all about *you*, you've stepped onto dangerous ground. You're probably losing your way. If you find yourself justifying your actions to yourself and others, red flags should be popping up like weeds.

As Arnold was preparing to hand over the plans to West Point, he must have been rationalizing his actions to himself. "I'm doing this terrible thing, but the reason is justified. They're *making* me do this because they overlooked my heroic service at the Battle of Saratoga and I was passed over for promotion. They schemed to bring down my whole career after I engaged in some harmless moneymaking ventures in Philadelphia." Arnold no doubt rationalized his treason by listing every perceived affront ever directed toward him.

Even an unsympathetic observer would agree that Arnold got a raw deal prior to his treason. But then, so did every other Revolutionary leader in this book. Washington, Jefferson, Adams, Hamilton...at one time or another, each of these men was subjected to scurrilous accusations, slanders, slights, abuse, and undeserved treatment at the hands of jealous rivals and hyper-competitive colleagues. The difference between Arnold and the men who became known as the Founding Fathers is that they recognized that the Revolution was *not* all about them, but about a larger and more worthy cause—a cause worth hardship and sacrifice.

All the Founding Fathers had a sense of self-service and concern for posterity, but ultimately, they all knew—all except for Arnold—that the Glorious Cause was not about them. They found a middle path between the extreme of egotism and self-aggrandizement on the one hand, and selfless behavior on the other.

The Founding Fathers found this middle path partly with considerable help from the "moral mentors" in their lives—someone Arnold apparently never had. Those mentors might have lived during their generation or might have been historical models such as Cicero, Plato, or Jesus. Regardless, the Founders had people who could objectively evaluate their actions and speak openly and honestly about them and to them. The Founders were able to consult with older and wiser people, who would also coach them on their roads to maturity, pointing out warning signs and "unworthy reasons." Without a mentor, Arnold had nobody to prop up his sense of self-worth, nobody to get in his face, nobody to correct his course when it veered toward the dark side. Without a mentor, he was left to blaze his own path through the moral jungle, and he failed. Like a child rationalizing selfish behavior, Arnold chose to justify his vainglory-seeking instead of knowing how to recognize and repudiate it.

Some historians have cast Arnold's wife Peggy in the role of a "Lady Macbeth," suggesting that she goaded Arnold to treason by whispering inflammatory remarks in his ear and appealing to his wounded pride. That may be true, but one has to ask why Arnold would have married such a woman in the first place. What does that say about his character, and why he would have felt compelled to accept such advice? Arnold was hardly a weak-minded puppet.

One is also left wondering whether Arnold would have behaved differently if he *had* received the plaudits and rewards he so desperately craved. Would that recognition have satisfied his ego? Would he have behaved any differently? Would he have betrayed another cause if not the cause of American independence and democratic self-government?

Of course he would have behaved *somewhat* differently. The question is, how much? There are people whose self-esteem can never receive enough care and feeding. Like a tapeworm, their egos are insatiable. At some point, Arnold would probably have betrayed the ideals of the Revolution, even if that betrayal manifested in ways less harmful to the war effort. Perhaps he would have participated in the Newburgh Conspiracy after the war, hoping to crown himself emperor. Maybe he would have tried to unseat Washington as commander-in-chief. Others had already tried it.

It is extremely difficult to consistently do the right thing for the wrong reasons; such behavior is not sustainable. You can get away with faux-noble behavior for a time—even a long time—but if your real motivation is stroking your ego or enriching yourself, you will eventually reveal your motivation to the world.

Realizing a vision often requires that we partner with other people. This can be for good if you partner with the *right people*. Proverbs 13:20 (TLB) says, "Be with wise men and become wise. Be with evil men and become evil." If you partner with another person to realize a vision that's ultimately about self-aggrandizement and ego enhancement, you may collaborate well for a while, but eventually your interests will diverge. Eventually, you'll find you aren't getting everything you need from the partner and you will go off in separate directions—and this divergence may or may not involve a betrayal of some sort. As 1 Corinthians 15:33 (NIV) says, "Bad company corrupts good character."

Are you seeking self, or are you seeking something greater than yourself?

The good leader must have a moral compass and take up a cause that jibes with the compass headings.

If it's a matter of self or others, what do you see when you look into the mirror? When Arnold looked in the mirror, he saw only himself reflected.

Some revisionist historians have pointed out that many of the Founding Fathers had selfish reasons for pursuing independence. Washington, for example, speculated in Western lands, as had many Virginia planters. There are suggestions that if the British hadn't forbidden the colonists from colonizing beyond the Alleghenies, men such as Hancock and Washington and Jefferson would have had little or no interest in independence. They might have said: *King George III is okay. Tax away without representation! We're making plenty of money.*

There's some measure of truth behind this argument. When you look at the early history of the colonies, you won't find anyone saying, "Hey, let's revolt. Let's go do our own thing." The early colonists had no reason to revolt. There was nothing in it for them. So you can point to selfish motivations that men such as Washington, Hancock, and Jefferson may have had for leading the Revolution, and you would not be entirely wrong. There's no question that some of their motivations were selfish.

Selfish economic motives can never adequately explain the words and deeds of these men. If expanding their merchant empires and their land holdings was the only (or even the prime) motivation for these men, then their subsequent behavior was pretty irrational. It doesn't make sense in terms of risks and rewards. Many of them risked their lives for the cause of independence. That's not something an affluent, intelligent businessman does—he doesn't gamble his life and fortune, his sacred honor, and his family's future on a spin of the roulette wheel. That is the hallmark of either an impulsive fool or someone dedicated to ideals that are greater than his own self-interest.

No, self-interest was hardly the only motivation for the decision to break from England, nor even the primary motivation. There was a higher cause associated with it, even though there was *some* enlightened self-interest involved.

It is the people who focus *only* on self who are eventually driven mad. It is the people who, like Arnold, search only for glory—instead of experiences bigger than themselves—who ultimately feel empty and betrayed.

A vision focused on self will always lead to inner bankruptcy. A vision built on serving others will not only serve society as a whole, but also nourish your own soul.

Back in 2008, Sara was a college senior playing for the championship of the Great Northwest Athletic Conference softball league. In the second inning of the game, she hit her first ever home run. The ball sailed right out of the park. While rounding the bases, however, she realized that she'd failed to touch first base. So she turned back. But through a twist of fate and of her knee, she found herself on the ground with a torn ligament, crawling in agony back to first base. According to the rules, she would have been out if anyone from her team had helped her.

That's when Mallory Holtman from the other team stepped up to help. She and her teammate, Liz Wallace, carried Sara around the bases, making sure to tap Sara's foot on each base. Though Mallory and Liz lost the game that day, they clearly accomplished something more important.[59]

Life is not about living for yourself. That is a guaranteed way to lose. Real significance comes when you live for something greater than yourself—when you live to make a difference in other people's lives. Benedict Arnold never learned this lesson and died searching for the significance that had always eluded him.

We have a choice. We can live for ourselves and, like Arnold, find ourselves on a never-ending quest for a purpose we never find. Or we can live for something greater than our personal wants and desires. It is *there* that we will find meaning, purpose, and significance.

CHAPTER SIX

LEWIS AND CLARK: MARCHING OFF THE MAP

A Roman general became engaged in a tremendous conflict that forced him into unexplored territory. Dispatching messengers back to Rome, the general made the following plea: "Send new orders, for we have marched off the map." [60]

AMERICA'S MOST FAMOUS EXPLORERS SET OUT on the journey of a lifetime, at the behest of President Thomas Jefferson, shortly after the Louisiana Purchase. Known as the Corps of Discovery, this band of handpicked U.S. Army volunteers was commanded by Captain Meriwether Lewis and his friend Second Lieutenant William Clark. The purpose of the journey, which lasted from May 1804 to September 1806, was to explore and map the newly acquired lands, find a practical route across the western half of the continent, and establish an American presence in the vast territory before Britain and other European powers could claim it. The Corps of Discovery was charged with studying the area's plants, animals, and geography, as well as establishing trade with the Indian tribes they encountered.

As leaders of the mission, Meriwether Lewis and William Clark would one day become synonymous with adventure and danger, opportunity, and raw courage.

Lewis served as the private secretary of Thomas Jefferson. Previously, he had served in the state militia and had helped quell the uprising known as the Whiskey Rebellion. While in the service, he crossed paths with William Clark, who had also spent much of his life in the state militia and U.S. Army. Later, Clark returned to his family's estate in Virginia to oversee the household and the land. In 1803, however, he received a letter from his old friend Lewis inviting him to experience a new adventure. Given his military background, his expertise in cartography, and his frontier experience, Clark was the perfect choice to join Lewis in leading this great and hazardous expedition.

WANTED: GREAT ORGANIZING SKILLS PATH

As the executors of a grand vision, Lewis and Clark were determined not just to survive, but to succeed in a vast and hostile environment. They were driven to go places none of their countrymen had been before.

Leaders who march off the map do so because they are adventurous, but also because they want to create a better future. The Wright brothers took to the skies because adventure and courage dwelled in their souls, but more importantly, they were trying to bring positive change to the world (or in their case, a tectonic shift).

There are many parallels between the journey of Lewis and Clark and the journeys of business leaders and family leaders (a.k.a. parents). Every day of our lives is an adventure. We admire those leaders who are always riding into the unknown. Like it or not, we have no choice but to ride into the unknown. Because we never know what the next day will bring, we are always planning for the next phase of the trek.

What distinguishes people who are actively striving to succeed from those who are satisfied with mere survival is *higher purpose*. The former have given themselves reasons to get up in the morning because they have created visions worth pursuing.

Another distinguishing characteristic of leaders versus followers is courage—the courage to try something new, whether that "something" is raising children or launching a new venture. Just as important, it also takes courage to *stop* doing something, to turn away from destructive impulses and actions, as well as limited perceptions and unproductive behavior.

Another parallel between the world of Lewis and Clark and the world in which we live now is this: Neither world was, or is, safe. The world can be a hostile place, so you had better be prepared. If Lewis and Clark had not prepared for their epic journey, Lewis would be an asterisk on history's list of people who served as aides to Thomas Jefferson, and Clark would be unknown.

It was the willingness of Lewis and Clark to go where no one else had gone (very few white men anyway) and how thoroughly they prepared for the quest that is worthy of both praise and emulation. In their era and in our own, most people never attempted to achieve much more than survival. The average person got up in the morning, went to work, worked, came home, and went to bed. The average person was part of the same "rat race" in the 19th century as we are today. They were simply coping with whatever obstacles life tossed in their path.

If you want to do something great with your life—if you want to lead your kids to greatness or achieve something worthwhile in the business community—you must be willing to take risks and march into uncharted territories. And you must take with you only what is needed for the journey. You must differentiate between proper planning and greed. You must also realize that the journey may be a lonely one, and it may even be a disappointing one. Lewis and Clark named one of their resting places "Camp Disappointment." I think everybody has found a Camp Disappointment at some point.

To achieve the ultimate vision, however, you must accept that loneliness and disappointment are part of the job. You must battle through these disappointments and feelings of isolation. The advantage that Lewis and Clark possessed (if you want to call it an advantage) is that there was no turning back. Separated from the United States by a distance of nearly a thousand miles (and that was just at the journey's start) they had little chance of being rescued if the mission met with disaster. They believed they had little choice but to move forward or die in the attempt, and their planning and preparation reflected this attitude.

Throughout history, some leaders have "burned their ships" after landing at the start of the journey to ensure that their men were motivated to press ahead or die trying. The Spanish conquistador Hernán Cortés *literally* burned his ships after arriving on Mexico's shores in 1519. Although failure is always a possibility, it was such an unattractive possibility for Cortés that he erased this option from his drawing board.

(I'm sure his men were surprised, but not especially delighted, by this ingenious motivational tactic.)

To achieve the kind of success that most people only dream of, the average business leader, the average parent, the average coach, the average schoolteacher must be willing to make sacrifices—to decide that they are *not* going to settle for average.

Instead, they must decide *I'm going to take my teammates to new places*. I'm going to take them places that transcend the mundane and the mediocre.

> *To conquer these new and potentially hostile environments, the leader should pack three pieces of equipment in addition to their long-term visions:*
>
> *Organizational skills*
>
> *Recruiting skills*
>
> *Courage*

GETTING YOUR ACT TOGETHER

Regarding organizational skills, insightful leaders ask themselves, "What will I need and when will I need it?" Just as importantly, they ask, "How can I prepare for the unexpected? How will I adjust my plans (and even improvise) if we encounter unexpected problems?"

On more than one occasion, the best-laid plans of Lewis and Clark were derailed by unforeseen circumstances. In the most famous example, a new form of portable boat, the design and construction of which Lewis fretted over for months, sank on its first launch. Only *after* the disaster did Lewis realize the cause of the problem—and by then it too late. Thereafter, he and his men had to build canoes (pirogues) from available trees as they were needed.

Lewis was chosen to lead Jefferson's expedition for many reasons, but chief among them was his knack for planning, organizing, and executing long-term strategies. As a fellow Virginia planter, Jefferson was impressed with Lewis' management skills and attention to detail, and described him as "assiduous and attentive...observing with minute attention all plants and insects he met with."

Jefferson's faith was well placed. From the very start of the expedition, Lewis was obsessed with research, planning, and organizing, with packing and repacking, with forecasting probabilities and possibilities, with plotting contingency courses to be followed in the event the original plans and strategies proved impossible to execute. From the very start, Lewis was determined to stay on top of circumstances—an attitude I analogize with staying on top of your mattress. Sometimes you may ask a person how they are doing and they reply, "Okay, I guess, under the circumstances." When I hear that, I often wonder, "What are you doing under the circumstances?" Circumstances are like a mattress. You have to stay on top of them. If you are under a mattress, you could be smothered to death. If you're on top of the mattress, you can rest peacefully. So it is with circumstances in life. Throughout the long journey, Lewis was committed to staying on top of the circumstances—a lesson we all should heed.

Obviously, leaders must stay "on top of the mattress" to have any hope of properly executing the vision. Toward this end, Lewis spent day after day and month after month reviewing and revising lists of food, supplies, and equipment needed for the journey in an effort to maximize the odds of success. He didn't want to waste time and precious energy hauling even a small piece of equipment if that equipment was not necessary for accomplishing the mission.

> Among other things, [Lewis] bought and had shipped to Wood River, where it was repacked for the expedition: 4,175 complete rations, at $14 each; 5,555 rations of flour at $.04 each; 100 gallons of whiskey at $1.28 each; 20 gallons of whiskey at $1 each; 4,000 rations of salt pork at $.04 each; plus ground corn and much more.[61]

Ironically, though, Lewis' meticulous planning could easily have backfired:

> *The Indians, they hoped, would be willing to talk and trade,*
> *but it would be the Indians' choice. They might decide to fight.*
> *Certainly they would be tempted. The expedition's arsenal was*
> *by far the biggest ever brought to the Missouri country, and any*
> *tribe able to take possession of it would dominate the region—*
> *no matter what the Louisiana Purchase said—for a long time*
> *to come.*[62]

Unfortunately for the men of the expedition, so little was known about the territory they were about to explore that no amount of planning could guarantee success. They were marching *very* far off the map. In fact, some of Lewis' and Jefferson's theories about the lands and peoples the expedition would encounter were ludicrous.

These tribes were virtually unknown except to a handful of British and French traders. There were many stories and rumors about them, mostly the Sioux, but little solid fact available.

Jefferson and Lewis had talked at length about the tribes on the basis of near-complete ignorance. They speculated that the lost tribe of Israel could be out there on the Plains, but it was more likely, in their minds, that the Mandans were a wandering tribe of Welshmen. Because they subscribed to such odd ideas, Jefferson's instructions to Lewis on how to deal with the tribes were, in most particulars, hopelessly naïve and impossible to carry out.[63]

In addition to acquiring necessary supplies, Lewis and Clark insisted on handpicking each member of the Corps after conducting a thorough screening. So determined were they that not a single slacker would be brought along for the ride, they rejected many more applicants than they accepted, and never hesitated to "fire" anyone who became more of a liability than an asset. Everyone had a vital part to play in the mission's success, and Lewis and Clark spent countless hours developing systems and organizing the men to ensure that no skill or talent would be wasted. Even before leaving St. Louis in May 1804, Lewis had them organized.

...divided the party into three squads, or 'messes,' which among other things would cook and eat together. Each evening, upon landing, Sergeant Ordway would hand out to each mess a day's provisions. It would be cooked at once, and apportion reserved for the following day. No cooking was allowed during the day. The regular ration was hominy and lard on one day, salt pork and flour the next, and cornmeal and pork the following day... Lewis' Detachment Order was exact about the responsibilities of the sergeants on the boat as it moved upstream. One sergeant was stationed at the helm, another midships, and the third in the bow. The sergeant at the helm steered, saw to the baggage on the quarterdeck, and attended the compass. The sergeant midships commanded the guard, managed the sails, saw that the men at the oars did their duty, and kept a good lookout for the mouths of all rivers, creeks, islands, and other remarkable places. He also measured out the whiskey ration and served as the sergeant-of-the-guard at night. The sergeant at the bow was charged to keep a good lookout, and to report all hunting camps or parties of Indians.[64]

Organizational skills are mandatory for leading your company, and your family, to new places. You must have vision and the ability to execute, but if you are not organized, the likelihood of seeing that vision to completion is greatly diminished. Not every boss has an aptitude for organization, in which case he or she had better find somebody who can handle that function. Such leaders should have an assistant help them with research, planning, and organizing. Otherwise, they won't know which side of the mattress is up.

Besides a lack of innate talent, another common impediment to organization is the leader who's too quick to say no to new ideas. It's a big mistake that leaders frequently make. They say no to ideas before they really know whether they ought to. They hear something "crazy" and immediately dismiss it. "We can't do that. We can't make *that* happen." They talk themselves out of fresh approaches and into behavioral loops—into trying the same failed strategies and tactics again and again.

NO SECRET FORMULA

I'm sometimes asked if there's a secret formula for consistently choosing the right people for the mission. My typical response is, "If I could come up with a secret formula, I'd scrap this book and write one about that formula so I could become an overnight millionaire." In other words, there is no secret formula.

However, a great blueprint is the one exemplified by the Lewis and Clark expedition.

Jefferson chose Lewis, Lewis chose Clark, and together Lewis and Clark handpicked the men who would join them. While en route, the Corps of Discovery enlisted the help (and sometimes leadership) of others who could help them realize the vision.

When I think about recruiting people to help one march off the map, my mind is always drawn to the great explorer Ernest Shackleton. In his search for a crew to go with him on a journey to Antarctica in 1914, Shackleton placed this want ad in the newspaper:

> *"Men wanted for hazardous journey. Low wages, bitter cold, long hours of complete darkness. Safe return doubtful. Honour and recognition in event of success."*

It took courage to go with Shackleton into the unknown in 1914, and what great courage it took for men to join Lewis and Clark as they marched off the map. Leaders must find people of great courage if they want their organization to go anywhere, much less into the great unknown.

Most of the men and women who later joined the expedition had already "gone part of the distance" to the Pacific, which offers us an important lesson. When entering uncharted territory, be sure to enlist the help of people who've already achieved *some* of your goals. For the most part, Lewis and Clark collected information from their own observations, but they also made inquiries of the locals whenever they could find any. "They asked questions of every Indian and white trader they met. These information-gathering sessions sometimes lasted a full day, occasionally even longer." Sacagawea (along with her husband) is the most famous of the locals who joined the Corps as an interpreter and source of intelligence about the paths that lay ahead.[65]

Lewis and Clark needed people who could provide a variety of skills. They needed people who could steer boats, people who could track game and hunt, and people who knew the lay of the land. They needed to fill particular skillsets with the right person. To paraphrase Jim Collins, they needed the right people in the right seat of the bus.

They couldn't possibly accomplish this mission by themselves. Although the Corps of Discovery was led by just two men, a team effort was needed to achieve Jefferson's vision.

Look for people within your organization, people you can trust— who aren't lazy. Laziness has been the death of more vision quests than any other factor. It doesn't matter what the project is, laziness will kill it every time. Your teammates and subordinates don't have to be the sharpest crayon in the box; they don't have to be the fastest runners or the strongest swimmers. The most important prerequisite is that they are willing to work hard. If you recruit lazy people, you can forget about the mission before you even begin.

If you're going to undertake a mission, if you're going to march off the map like Lewis and Clark, you must be brave and you must recruit people who are brave...and smart. They don't have to be book-smart. It's more important that they be street-smart. Sometimes you need people in an organization who don't necessarily have advanced degrees, but who know how to execute a plan—fearlessly. You need people who intuitively "get" what you are trying to accomplish and will quickly adopt your vision as *their* vision.

Throughout this book, I've referred to the head, the heart, and the gut. The leader should use all three tools, especially when selecting people for the job. The leader must use his head and his heart to figure out whether the talent pool contains the right people for the mission. But in the end, he must listen to his gut. Ultimately, let your intuition be your guide.

Like Lewis and Clark, you should seek out people who have traveled part of the way. Keep in mind, however, that some of these people will have gone only part of the way because they attempted to achieve what you're attempting and didn't succeed—and some may be bitter about their failures. Hence, you may encounter a modern-day Sacagawea who tries to discourage you from going the distance while you're gleaning information from her. *This* is where strength and the clarity of purpose come into play.

Listening is also a vital skill. Most leaders want to be the center of attention, but wise leaders spend more time listening than talking. Calvin Coolidge once said, "It takes a great man to become a good listener." Don't expect what you hear to always match your preconceptions. Be open to ideas that may blow your mind...if you give them a chance.

Parents naturally want to tell their kids what to do. *I'm the boss of the family. I run the show. This is what you need to do.* But good parents listen to their kids; they really listen to what their children have to say. I think leaders must fight the natural urge to always be the center of attention. Stephen Covey said, "Most people do not listen with the intent to understand; they listen with the intent to reply." Leaders must set aside their egos while looking for people who can give them the next scrap of information—a clue, a warning, or the inspiration needed to continue the journey.

The way to find the people you'll need is to keep your antenna up. Whatever you do, don't assume that insights and information can come from only a handful of sources—e.g., "I'm only going to listen to people in my field." The people you need may work outside your industry.

While writing this book, for example, I met someone who was also writing a book—someone a little farther down the road on this literary journey—so I asked him, "What have you learned in the process?" I learned more in the short time I listened to him than I ever thought possible. You never know where or when you might find valuable information.

Good leaders keep their radar on at all times. Lewis and Clark found people in unusual places and at times when they weren't looking for help. They didn't say, "Hey, let's get in the boat and go see if we can find an Indian interpreter to help us." But they were smart enough to employ her talents (some of the time) once they met up with her.

THE DEFINITION OF COURAGE

According to Ambrose Redmoon, "Courage is not the absence of fear but rather the judgment that something else is more important than fear."

That really resonates with me.

People with courage are not fearless. In fact, it's impossible to possess courage unless you have experienced and understand the meaning of fear. Otherwise, your actions are the result of ignorance—of not knowing enough about the world to realize that you *do* have reasons to be afraid. Overcoming fear, realizing that some things in life are so important that you must tuck away your fear and proceed anyway: that requires genuine courage. Real bravery.

Mountains are not climbed and winters are not survived without courage. You never arrive at wonderful new places without courage.

I've visited Fort Clatsop, where the Corps ended its voyage to the Pacific. It's a beautiful place, but one they would never have reached if everyone hadn't had courage. You've got to have courage to see opportunity, and you've got to have courage to overcome the obstacles.

Courage calculates the costs. Courage requires measured thinking.

Foolhardiness does none of these things.

The foolish person is one who says, "I don't care. I'm going to play chicken with this other car going 100 miles per hour, and call that courage." Foolhardiness throws good judgment and discretion out the window, whereas courage involves measured thinking.

Foolhardiness is ignorance and stupidity in action. Courage puts calculated risks into motion.

Of course, it can sometimes be difficult to tell the difference between foolhardiness and courage—very difficult. Most business leaders aren't the skydiving and extreme snowboarding types, but sometimes the outward manifestations of courage—their actual behaviors—can appear foolish. That's why leaders must constantly take readings and perform measurements. They must constantly calculate the risks and think matters through. If a particular course of action scares you, that's okay. *That* is when courage must be summoned.

At the risk of redundancy, this is another reason leaders should seek out advisors and mentors. These people can help them summon courage when it's most needed. Mentors are not just for the young. Oftentimes, people think mentorship has to do with taking young students under their wings, "I've got to tell this lad how to make it in life." All great leaders have relied on trusted advisors, people who show them the difference between measured thinking and thoughtless plowing ahead.

Even more important, leaders must summon the courage to *hear* the truth when that truth is spoken. They must have courage to let their egos be bruised by giving subordinates the freedom to speak plainly. Between Lewis and Clark, it was clear that Lewis was in charge. He was the one who assigned the tasks. But he allowed Clark to speak to him, to disagree with him, to cut through the clutter that sometimes clouded his mind. (Many historians believe Lewis suffered from clinical depression.) Many of history's great decisions have been made because the leaders surrounded themselves with a "think tank" of wise advisors. Proverbs 15:22 (NLT) says, "Plans go wrong for lack of advice; many advisers bring success."

Think back to the war councils that Washington convened whenever major military decisions had to be made. As often as not, subordinates would talk the great commander out of decisions he was determined to make. Sometimes he didn't listen to them, and everyone still did their best to execute his plans. At other times, times when Washington had deluded himself into believing, "By golly, we're going to go back into the field and somehow beat those redcoats," his advisors responded, "Whoa there, General Washington, that's very courageous but also dumb. We'll get slaughtered. Do the most courageous thing possible and step away. Let's fight on our terms and on a battlefield of our choosing instead of bravely charging the enemy and getting ourselves mowed down by musket fire."

The courage to listen to advice that doesn't please you isn't easy, but it's critical. It's not poor leadership or weakness. Rather, it's wisdom in action. When interviewed in the Ken Burns documentary *The Civil War*, the late historian Shelby Foote talked about how much courage it would have taken for Confederate General James Longstreet to cancel the final Confederate assault at Gettysburg, known as Pickett's Charge. Shelby said, "Nobody has that much courage." If only Longstreet had been able to muster the courage, thousands of Southern men might have lived to see another day.

ONCE THE SHOOTING BEGINS, PLANS ARE WORTHLESS

One of Dwight Eisenhower's favorite sayings was that in "war, before the battle is joined, plans are everything, but once the shooting begins, plans are worthless." (The less noble Mike Tyson once said, "Everyone has a plan until they get punched in the face.") The same can be said about exploration. In battle, what cannot be predicted is the enemy's reaction; in exploration, what cannot be predicted is what is around the next bend in the river or on the other side of the mountain. The planning process, therefore, is as much guesswork as it is intelligent forecasting of the physical needs of the expedition. It can be frustrating, because the planner carries with him a nagging sense that he is making some simple mistake that could be easily corrected in the planning stage, but may cause a dead loss when the mistake is discovered midway through the voyage.[66]

However meticulous and well-considered your plans, as hard as you've tried to recruit people who are smart and detail-oriented, you also need people who can play any position in a pinch. When you're marching off the map, everyone's role is going to change: The plans have become worthless, and the only reasonable response is to improvise. You may have been the cook three minutes ago, but now you're the one who's got to stand up in the boat and defend against an Indian attack.

As a leader, it's necessary to surround yourself with people who are expert in their field and specialized function, but it's also important to surround yourself with people who can assume new roles and responsibilities when everything starts to go south...when you march off the map and discover that people's résumés are no longer worth the paper they're printed on.

Exploration is unpredictable.

Even the leader who's a genius in one field must become broader than the one field.

Bill Gates may have started his career as a nerd who made computers in his garage, but he *grew* to become the CEO of a multi-billion-dollar enterprise. His vision had to expand for Microsoft to become bigger. Otherwise he'd still be tinkering with motherboards in the garage.

Steve Jobs is another example of broadening and growth, as is Mark Cuban, owner of the Dallas Mavericks. (Cuban also got his start in computers.) Steve Jobs, Bill Gates, Mark Cuban...they can all sit and talk about wiring and batteries and megahertz and bytes, but to lead gigantic organizations they had to grow as human beings, inspiring people to build something greater than the small organizations they first launched.

When it comes to family, too, I think somebody, whether it's mom or dad, must be charting a course for the family. *Where are we going to go, what are we going to do?* And somebody in the family should be dealing with all the details. *What time are we picking up Brayden from football practice, and Briley from volleyball, and then taking Berkeley to cheer practice?* Families need people with vision and people who can execute. If they don't, they're liable to start drifting. Focus and flexibility are important keys to marching off the map.

I think we've become too focused as leaders and as a society on the power and prestige of experts and specialists, ignoring the value that "general practitioners" can bring to the table.

The GP looks to the patient's *total health*, not just curing specific illnesses but preventing them, whereas specialists, rather than addressing the needs of the entire body, are sometimes too focused on details. The value that the GP provides is that she keeps her eyes on the proverbial 30,000-foot perspective.

If you visit the Mayo Clinic, you'll discover that you don't work with 50 doctors; you'll see one doctor—the leader of a team that covers a variety of disciplines. The leader brings in the players needed for the occasion. This makes sense. If you or a loved one needs treatment, would you want to be examined by just one specialist, or would you rather work with a team led by someone who always has her eyes on the big picture—someone who won't treat every condition as a nail in need of a hammer?

Lewis and Clark were great explorers, but it didn't happen by accident. These men worked hard to achieve their goals and were willing to go where no one else like them had ever been. These men loved adventure and dreamed of what the uncharted territory would hold. Their courage must be our courage if we expect to take our organization or families into uncharted waters. As leaders, we must be organized and surround ourselves with people who will help us achieve shared goals. But, most importantly, we must have the heart of the lion. The word "courage" comes to us in English from the Latin root word *cor*, meaning heart. Great leaders have great courage—they have heart.

Take heart, leader! You are about to march off the map.

CONCLUSION

THIS BOOK HAS BEEN FOCUSED ON the big picture. One of my goals has been to reinforce George Santayana's quote, "Those who cannot learn from history are doomed to repeat it." But there are two other notable quotes that run true throughout this book. Regarding marching off the map, Ralph Waldo Emerson said, "Do not go where the path may lead, go instead where there is no path and leave a trail." Regarding mentors and advisors, Isaac Newton said, "If I have seen farther than others, it is because I was standing on the shoulders of giants." The person leading today stands on the shoulders of those who followed similar courses in the past. That's how humanity works.

Did Genghis Khan read biographies of other world leaders? Was he even aware that they existed? I have no idea. But I guarantee there was somebody who inspired him when he was young, and there were experiences that taught him valuable lessons. The important thing to understand and adopt is the notion of *lifelong learning*. That term has become popular in the business world over the past decade. In fact, because it's very much in vogue, I worry it will soon become a cliché that reputable thought leaders deride simply because it's become so trendy.

If that happens, the world will have lost a precious nugget of wisdom.

We shouldn't graduate from high school, college, or graduate school and announce (to ourselves) that we are finished learning. Great leaders choose to continue learning because they recognize that we must always be learning to move forward.

We must be lifelong learners, or arrogance will come to dominate our personalities and our lives. We will fool ourselves into thinking that we know all there is to know—that we've been there and done that, "so don't waste my time with ideas and facts that don't fit my preconceptions." In short, not only will we *not* know what we don't know, we will refuse to learn what we don't know.

You may be good. You may even be great. But you will never be as great as you could be if you call a premature halt to the lifelong journey of learning—if you refuse to learn from your experiences and those of others. If you're not reading about the lives of history's greatest leaders, you're not trying to reach your full potential.

If Dallas Cowboys' quarterback Roger Staubach needed a mentor like Tom Landry, and "the great one" Michael Jordan needed Bulls' coach Phil Jackson, then each of us needs a mentor in our lives. Sometimes coaches are people who can directly address our lives and sometimes they are people who have long since died.

Though they may no longer be alive, history's great leaders still have voices with which they can speak to us and teach us. The question is, are you listening?

ENDNOTES

1 Brands, H.W. *Benjamin Franklin: The Original American*, lecture series by H.W. Brands, Barnes and Noble Audio, 2003, 7 CDs.

2 Ibid.

3 Carnegie, D. (1981). *How to Win Friends and Influence People.* New York: Pocket Books, xvi.

4 Bolton, R. (1979). *People Skills.* New York: Simon & Schuster, p. 7.

5 Wheatley, M. J. (2002). *Turning to One Another: Simple Conversations to Restore Hope to the Future.* San Francisco: Berrett-Koehler Publishers, Inc., p. 19.

6 McCullough, D. (2001). *John Adams.* New York: Simon & Schuster, pp. 208-209.

7 Jackson, E. (2012, June 16). "89 Business Clichés That Will Get Any MBA Promoted And Make Them Totally Useless." *Forbes*, June 16, 2012.

8 Inscription from a church in Sussex, England, written in 1730.

9 bartleby.com

10 Ellis, J. (1998). *American Sphinx.* New York: Vintage Books, p. 54.

11 Ibid, p. 63.

12 Ibid, p. 244.

13 Ibid, p. 249.

14 Ellis, J. (2001). *Founding Brothers.* New York: Alfred A. Knopf, p. 34.

15 The Necessity of a Real Vision—bit.ly/192PH30

16 Pflaeging, N., Hermann, S., Vollmer, L., & Carvalho, V. (2012, June). "Organize for Complexity." BetaCodex Network White Paper No. 12.

17 Elson, H. W. (1904). *History of the United States of America*. New York: The MacMillan Company, p. 258-265.

18 SportsDayDFW.com, "Mike Ditka: If It weren't for Tom Landry, 'I'd probably be tending bar." *SportsDayDFW.com* May 24, 2013.

19 Paine, T. (1776, December 23). *The American Crisis*.

20 history.org/almanack/life/manners/rules2.cfm

21   Ellis, J. J. (2005). *His Excellency: George Washington*. Vintage, p. 17.

22 Ellis, J. J. (2001). *Founding Brothers*. New York: Alfred A. Knopf, p. 130.

23 Ibid.

24 Wood, G. S. (2006). *Revolutionary Characters*. New York: The Penguin Press, p. 43.

25 Ibid, p. 44.

26 Fischer, D. (2005). *Washington's Crossing*. New York: Oxford University Press.

27 Freeman, D. (1968). *Washington*. New York: Touchstone, p. 517.

28 Ellis, J. (2004). *His Excellency: George Washington*. New York: Alfred A. Knopf, p. 272.

29 Winik, J. (2007). *The Great Upheaval*. New York: Harper, p. 505.

30 Wood, G. (2006). *Revolutionary Characters: What Made the Founders Different*. New York: The Penguin Press, p. 177.

31 McCullough, D. (2001). *John Adams*. New York: Simon & Schuster, p. 144.

32 Ibid, p. 40.

33 Ibid, p. 66.

34 John Adams, diary entry. March 5, 1773.

35 McCullough, p. 89.

36 Ibid, p. 126-127.

37 Merryman, A. (2013, September 24). Losing Is Good for You. *New York Times.*

38 Winik, p. 543.

39 The actual year of Hamilton's birth is in question. Hamilton himself claimed 1757, but substantial evidence points to 1755.

40 Historians believe Hamilton intentionally fired above Burr's head to settle the duel without bloodshed, expecting Burr to follow suit.

41 Chernow, R. (2005). *Alexander Hamilton.* New York: The Penguin Press, p. 320.

42 Ibid, pp. 321-322.

43 Ibid, pp. 328-329

44 Ibid, pp. 249-250

45 beinkandescent.com/tips-for-entrepreneurs/461/business-tips-from-the-love-doctor

46 Chernow, p. 4.

47 ushistory.org/us/10f.asp

48 Stoll, I. (2008). *Samuel Adams: A Life.* New York: Free Press, p. 42.

49 Ibid, p. 43.

50 Ibid, pp. 123-125.

51 Ibid, p. 83.

52 Miller, J. (2010). *The Revolutionary Paul Revere.* Nashville: Thomas Nelson, p. 144.

53 Garber, M. (2013, September). The Way We Lie Now. *The Atlantic Monthly.*

54 mfa.org/collections/object/sons-of-liberty-bowl-39072

55 Revere, P. (1961). *Paul Revere's Three Accounts of His Famous Ride.* Boston: Massachusetts Historical Society.

56 Boatner, M. M. (1975). *Encyclopedia of the American Revolution.* (Volume III). New York: David McKay.

57 Creighton, L. (2008, June 27). Benedict Arnold: A traitor, but once a patriot. *U.S. News.*

58 history.com/topics/benedict-arnold

59 http://bit.ly/eeTnPB

60 Taylor, B. (1996). *21 Truths, Traditions, and Trends.* Nashville: Convention Press, p. 178.

61 Ambrose, S. (1997). *Undaunted Courage.* New York: Touchstone.

62 Ibid.

63 Ibid.

64 Ibid.

65 Ibid.

66 Ibid, p. 81

ACKNOWLEDGMENTS

B EN FRANKLIN FAMOUSLY QUIPPED, "If Jack's in love, he's no judge of Jill's beauty." Over the past five years of writing, I have fallen in love with the "Jill" that is this book. I needed people to come alongside me and help me correctly judge her looks. The beauty of this book is due largely to the people listed in these acknowledgments.

From the beginning, I must acknowledge that I am leaving people out. For that, I am deeply sorry, but eternally grateful.

There were two friends in particular who helped make this book possible. The support and investment of Wally Gomaa and Tony Bridwell made this book come alive. Thank you for thinking with me, arguing opposing points of view, spurring me on, and helping make this book a reality. Also, thanks to Mickey Broach and Philip King for your input on content and design.

I began work over five years ago on this book, but without the help of my friend, writing coach, sounding board, interviewer, and editor Pete Gerardo, I'm sure the book would not have been completed for at least another five years. Thank you Pete for serving as an "Alexander Hamilton" who helped me execute the vision for the pages that follow. And thank you Kelly Andersson for pushing me across the finish line. Thank you to my friends at Elevate Publishing for your support and expertise which brought this piece of my heart into publication.

I want to also thank my friends at Dallas Baptist University. I am honored to teach U.S. History to great students, and appreciate the support of my colleagues in the history department. In particular, thanks to Dr. Adam Wright, Dr. Gary Cook, Dr. Greg Kelm, and Dr. Mike Williams—for your constant support and encouragement.

I am grateful to my dearest friends, staff, and members of FBC Carrollton and Church at The Fields. I am grateful for your support and am honored to journey through life with you. Many of the leadership lessons I share in this book have come from your influence in my life. Thank you for working with me to accomplish the vision before us.

I would not have been able to write this book without the support of my family. Thank you to my parents for instilling in me a great love for history. My love for our nation's proud history comes from many vacations as a child to historical sites from our country's past.

My wife Allison and my three children Berkeley, Briley, and Brayden have continued to support me when Dad had to "work on the book." Thank you for your patience and understanding while Dad completed this long project. "I have no greater joy than to know my children walk in the truth." 3 John 4 (NIV).

For all these people and many others not named, I am deeply indebted. All the good you glean from this book comes from their influence—and any errors are mine.

I close with some more wisdom from Benjamin Franklin:

Write to Please Yourself.
When You Write to Please Others
You End Up Pleasing No One.

This book has been in my heart for a long time and I am so very pleased to finally have it on paper. I hope it helps you be a better leader in your home and office. Our culture needs leadership like never before. May the lessons of the past cause us to look forward to an even greater future.

Brent Taylor, April 2017

ABOUT THE AUTHOR

Brent Taylor, D.Min., is a pastor, international speaker, professor of American history, and corporate communicator. He enjoys reading great stories from history, fishing, traveling, and helping people find their purpose in life. His other great passion is discovering the red light on at Krispy Kreme Donuts. Brent lives in the Dallas area with his wife and three children.

More information and contact details for speaking engagements are available online at DrBrentTaylor.com.

elevate
publishing

DELIVERING TRANSFORMATIVE MESSAGES
TO THE WORLD

Visit www.elevatepub.com for our latest offerings.

NO TREES WERE HARMED IN THE MAKING OF THIS BOOK.

Okay, so a few did make the ultimate sacrifice.

In order to steward our environment, we are partnered with *Plant With Purpose*, to plant a tree for every tree that paid the price for the printing of this book.

To learn more, visit www.elevatepub.com/about

PLANT W TH PURPOSE | WWW.PLANTWITHPURPOSE.ORG

CPSIA information can be obtained
at www.ICGtesting.com
Printed in the USA
BVHW01s0904190118
505662BV00029B/429/P